Let Me Heal You
Author Ni

Let Me Heal You © 2024 Author Ni

All rights reserved.

No part of this publication may be reproduced, stored in a retrieval system, or transmitted, in any form or by any means, electronic, mechanical, photocopying, recording or otherwise, without the prior written permission of the presenters.

Author Ni asserts the moral right to be identified as author of this work.

Presentation by *BookLeaf Publishing*

Web: www.bookleafpub.com

E-mail: info@bookleafpub.com

ISBN: 9789363309326

First edition 2024

*"In the crowd of ruthless mafias and rich businessmen,
Would you choose to fix a broken soul?"*

Contents

1. Chapter 1   1
2. Chapter 2   4
3. Chapter 3   6
4. Chapter 4   10
5. Chapter 5   13
6. Chapter 6   15
7. Chapter 7   18
8. Chapter 8   21
9. Chapter 9   24
10. Chapter 10   29
11. Chapter 11   33
12. Chapter 12   39
13. Chapter 13   44
14. Chapter 14   49
15. Chapter 15   54
16. Chapter 16   59
17. Chapter 17   65
18. Chapter 18   69

19. Chapter 19 — 73
20. Chapter 20 — 77
21. Chapter 21 — 82
22. Chapter 22 — 85
23. Chapter 23 — 90
24. Chapter 24 — 94
25. Chapter 25 — 97
26. Chapter 26 — 101
27. Chapter 27 — 105
28. Chapter 28 — 110
29. Chapter 29 — 115
30. Chapter 30 — 119
31. Chapter 31 — 124
32. Chapter 32 — 128
33. Chapter 33 — 133
34. Chapter 34 — 140
35. Chapter 35 — 145
36. Chapter 36 — 150
37. Chapter 37 — 155
38. Chapter 38 — 159
39. Chapter 39 — 164
40. Chapter 40 — 169
41. Chapter 41 — 174
42. Chapter 42 — 179

43.	Chapter 43	184
44.	Chapter 44	189
45.	Chapter 45	194
46.	Chapter 46	198
47.	Chapter 47	203
48.	Chapter 48	208
49.	Chapter 49	213
50.	Chapter 50	217
51.	Chapter 51	220
52.	Chapter 52	224
53.	Chapter 53	230
54.	Chapter 54	234
55.	Chapter 55	239
56.	Chapter 56	245
57.	Chapter 57	250
58.	Chapter 58	255
59.	Chapter 59	261
60.	Chapter 60	266
62.	Epilogue	274

I t's a story time.......

A boy was weakly standing in the middle of nowhere, he was pierced with lots of arrows in his back which were coming out from his chest. He was in extreme pain but still was trying to stand still. He had lots of wounds on his body and was already fragile.

But then, he saw a glimmer, a light....or something which was soothing his heart..... a face. He saw a girl with broken wings walking towards him. She seemed lost but still she had that charm which was calming him. Seeing that soft smile on her face, he gulped. "Are you ok?" she asked approaching him.

"No, stay away, or this will hurt you," he said, pointing at those sharp arrows in his chest to alert her. But she looked at him worriedly and said, "It's ok, I'll remove them for you. These look so painful."

"No! Please don't come near me." He was scared that his arrows might hurt her. He seemed so scared and weak. She slowly stepped towards him, and tears filled in his eyes, "It will be so painful."

"Trust me, you will be fine, I can't see you like this," she said looking into his eyes to calm him down.

She still slowly stepped near him; his arrows were touching her. She gently held his hand and he closed his eyes, it was calming him, and he was not feeling the pain anymore. Gaining his trust, she moved closer to him, letting those arrows poke her and eventually pierce through her body. She was feeling that pain but still she hugged him.

"Please don't hurt yourself," he cried. "I will make everything fine," she replied, slowly caressing his head to comfort him. She hugged him to feel his pain because she had no other option but to convince herself to let him get hurt more to free him from those traumatic things. She made her next move and slowly touched one of the arrows in his back and pulled it out from both of their bodies, they both screamed in pain. The process was even more painful but one by one she removed all those arrows. It was not like he was not enough strong to remove those arrows himself but all his strength was being spent on enduring that pain. She helped him because she had not been enduring that pain for years like him, so it was easier for her to bear it. But it was that fondness in his eyes for her, like even though he was in immense pain, he was still worried about *her*. That gave her the courage to make this move her destination. With his affection, which she had craved from feeling so alone, she felt no longer lost.

And they were just standing there, holding each other, caressing each other and healing each other with Love......

- Miss Ni

"*I'm broken.....*"
      "*I'm misery.....*"
"*But I find peace in your face*"

"**Then give me a chance to pull you into life again**"
"**I promise, I'll fix you**"

"*Don't try to fix me, you'll hurt yourself*"

"**If by hurting myself I can fix you, then I'm ready to get hurt**"
"**Trust me, I'll fix your shattered parts**"

"*Just let me feel you.... LET ME HEAl YOU.....*"

Chapter 1

She was panting hard.......
   Her legs were giving up........
But she could still hear the sound of running footsteps behind her. She glanced over her shoulder and tried to walk faster but ended up falling to her knees. Holding onto a nearby pole, she again stood up. That huge wedding dress she was wearing was giving her a hard time running. She forced herself to move, to step forward and protect herself, but her weak and tired body was of no help at all, and she collapsed once again.

"There she is!"

Her heart exploded hearing the voice.

That's it.

It's the end.

She looked behind and saw those men approaching her, but she had no more strength to run away from them. She again tried to stand up but ended up on the ground.

Today, Cera was supposed to get married, but she'd sneaked out of the ceremony. She refused to get married to the man her dad had chosen for her and being a stubborn soul, she couldn't sacrifice her freedom just like that. It was not marriage but more like a business deal. So, she ran away, leaving everything behind. She didn't care about her father, his prestige, or the deal that was suffocating her to death.

Yes, she ran away to catch a breath from her suffocating surroundings but now she was still out of breath while running away from those dirty drunk guys who just found her alone and started to chase her. Losing her way, she ended up in a dark alley, and now the men were in front of her.

"Now, where are you planning to run?" One of them said and grabbed Cera's wrist. Seeing his dirty smirk, she got chills down her spine.

"Leave me! Do you know who I am?" Cera yelled while trying to get out of his grip.

"I'm Cera Fo—" she gulped hard at her words, realizing something.

"You are a bride who's gonna have her first night with us instead of her groom," they both laughed wickedly, making Cera feel disgusted and weak.

Cera wasn't a weak girl, but this kind of situation can make anyone feel helpless and Cera also had no physical strength to fight back.

She flinched when one of them started to rip off the net fabric of her dress. Her heart raced, and the regret of leaving her father was visible on her face. She was scared.

"What are you doing? Leave me!" She was struggling to move them away.

Her voice echoed through the alley as they began to touch her exposed skin. Her eyes widened when one of them covered her mouth. She started to feel breathless. She bit down hard on his hand, and he quickly moved away groaning in pain. Cera cried out loudly, "HELP! SOMEBODY HELP ME! PLEASE SAVE M—"

But a hard slap landed on her cheek. Her vision began to blur as the men shoved her to the ground.

"Stop....p-please...d-don't-" Tears rolled down her face, and after closing her eyes, she couldn't feel anything but the darkness swallowing her.

But then.....

"Hey! What's going on here?" a voice interrupted them.

Chapter 2

He was alone again. It's fine, he guessed. The world was shiny enough, so he didn't bother to show his glow ever because he was scared. Scared of the bad eyes of the cruel world. What if he glows and the world mixes him with those other glowing things? He'll vanish again. They will use his glow to decorate their world and throw him away one day after he becomes of no use for them.

Jimmy was done with all his food deliveries so he was going home while thinking about his miserable life, but suddenly he heard a scream and he followed those noises coming from the alley nearby him. He stopped when he saw from afar that two guys were doing some bad things to a girl, his fist clenched but he decided to be calm.

"Hey! What's going on there?" Jimmy said while walking towards them. He had his phone holding in front like he was recording a video.

"You better mind your own business," one of them said showing him a knife.

"You're live streaming to Officer Parker's Office. Show your knife this way—yeah, like that." Jimmy angled his phone to focus on the knife.

"What? Just go away kid, you don't want to get in trouble." The man tried to grab Jimmy's phone, but he was fast enough to move away and said, "No way! 30k people are watching you. If you do somet—"

One of the bad men was about to attack Jimmy but then they heard a police siren. Jimmy sighed internally seeing those men running away and hiding their faces. Jimmy looked at his phone which had a broken camera but was enough to scare them and fortunately, that police siren also helped unexpectedly.

Jimmy pushed his hair back, feeling relieved but still shaken by the sight of the knife. He glanced at the unconscious figure of a girl in her torn wedding dress but he turned on his way without bothering to take her to a safe place. Walking a little further he stopped and sighed, rolling his eyes and again came back to her. He knelt to take a look at her.

For some reason, Jimmy couldn't stop staring at her. He tilted his head to get a closer look, removed some sticky hairs from her face and wiped that blood from the corner of her lips with his thumb. When he noticed her torn clothes, he looked away. Her body parts were exposed from the torn parts of her clothes. Without hesitation, Jimmy removed his hoodie and put it on her before carefully lifting her into his arms. Still, he was not able to take his eyes off her calm face.

Chapter 3

Jimmy brought the unknown girl to his house, where his mom was waiting for him all worried. Jimmy opened the door and entered while carrying her. As soon as his mom heard the sounds, she stood up.

"Jimmy?" She called out and Jimmy hummed in response to assure his mom that it was him.

"It's too late Jimmy, where were—" She stumbled on the chair in front of her and was about to fall but she again held onto the same chair.

"Mom, be careful!" He put the girl gently on the couch and went to check on his mom. He helped her sit down, holding her hand.

"Are you ok?" he asked, checking her leg. His mom waved her hands in the air to find his face. Jimmy took her hand and put it on his cheek.

She was blind.

"I'm fine. Why are you late? And have you brought someone?" she asked, sensing someone's presence.

"Y-Yes," he said, looking at the unconscious girl lying on the couch.

"I-Is she a g-girl?" she asked hesitantly as she had noticed that girly fragrance on her son.

"Yes, Mom," he said, putting his hand on her. But she pulled her hand back, her heart trembling.

"Why did you bring her?" Her tone was cold.

"Mom, s-she was....I didn't mean to bring her here but I th-thought leaving her there would be dangerous." Jimmy told his mom all that had happened in the alley.

"Oh my god! Is she fine?" she asked, concerned.

"Yes, but she is unconscious," he said, going towards the girl and again carrying her.

"What are you doing?" his mom asked again after some moments.

"I'm taking her to the room."

"Why?"

"Don't worry, I'll come back soon and I'll sleep here on the couch." He replied but her heart again clenched because he sounded cold. She felt a little bad.

"I mean-d-don't....Jimmy? Jimmy?" but before she completed herself, he was gone from there.

His mom was waiting for him to come back. After leaving the girl in the room, Jimmy came back and his mom felt his presence again.

"Jimmy, I'm sorry.... I didn't me-"

"Have you eaten anything, Mom?" Jimmy asked, completely ignoring her words as he searched for something.

"Yes, I had some pancakes, there are some for you also. I'll make some soup for that girl." Sometimes, she managed to cook by guessing the ingredients.

He didn't say anything as he found what he wanted and turned to go....

"Say something, Jimmy," she said, moving her hands in the air to find her son. Jimmy held her hand.

She gulped and held him by the shoulders and said, "Say something Jimmy, Shall I make something for you also? Will you eat? Or sh—"

"Mom, she has some bruises, I'm just going to treat her. Don't worry, I won't do anything to her, if you want, then you can come with me." Her heart shattered more hearing her son. A sharp wave of guilt went through her heart.

Jimmy slowly removed her hands and was about to leave, but she hugged him. "I'm sorry my son. I didn't mean it, I'm just scared," she said while crying.

Jimmy's tears also fell which he had been holding all this time because his own mother didn't trust him completely. But he wiped his tears, "It's OK, M-Mom, let's go if you want." He held her hand to guide her toward the room but she stopped wiping her tears, "No, I'll make something for her and you." She turned around finding her way to the kitchen.

"Are you sure, Mom?" Jimmy asked because he knew it would be a little hard for her.

"Yeah, I'll do it. Don't worry," she replied and walked away, while Jimmy also went back to check on the girl.

Jimmy returned to the girl again. He sprinkled some water on her face to wake her up. She just flinched but couldn't get conscious completely, so he started to treat her. She was wearing his hoodie but he was hesitant to remove it so he just treated the wounds on her face and head. He closed the aid box and sat beside her.

Jimmy was not like the other guys his age who liked to enjoy their lives by doing drugs and having fun. He had lived his life before his proper age, he had experienced and suffered more than a boy of his age should have.

He was misery....

He was broken....

And now he was finding some kind of peace in the girl's face. He was again staring at her with his blank eyes. But he was interrupted by the sound of the opening door.

"Jimmy, I think I messed up something in the kitchen. Will you please help?" His mom came, asking for help.

"I told you, it's OK, I'll do it. Stay here if you want to," he said and went out.

Jimmy's mom sat on the edge of the bed, reaching out for the girl's hand and caressing it.

"I don't know who you are but I hope you are fine."

Chapter 4

Cera felt her throat dry. Her eyelids felt too heavy to lift. Her sight was still blurry. She saw someone sitting near her while holding her hand. She gulped and blinked to clear her vision. And sudden memories of the time before she passed out started to play in her mind. Her hold tightened on the hand which was holding her. Tears started streaming down her face, thinking about the drunk men and their hands on her. Unconsciously, she sobbed.

"Oh, you are up dear?" Cera heard some lady's voice but she was still crying.

Cera felt the lady cupping her face. "Sweetie, are you crying? Aren't you feeling well?" the lady asked knowing Cera might be scared after the incident.

"Where a-am I-I?" Cera's voice trembled as she was hitching on her breath while crying.

"Mom, is she up?"

"Yes Jimmy, but she's crying."

Cera heard the conversation between that lady and a boy. She didn't know who these people were or how they were here. She was just crying while closing her eyes. They were looking at her not knowing how to calm her. And Cera's next question made them realize why she was crying.....

"W-what happened t-to me?" Cera squeezed her eyes, hopelessly holding on to the small pendant on her neck.....

"You are fine. Nothing happened to you, you were saved before something could have happened," Cera heard the boy saying and her sobs started to fade. She slowly opened her eyes to find a beautiful boy and that lady who was probably his mother.

"Yes dear, my son saved you on time, don't worry. You are fine and safe," the woman said, caressing Cera's hand.

Cera sighed in relief, "T-Thank you," she said trying to sit up so the lady helped her. Cera felt a little weird about the lady as she was moving her hands in the air.

"She can't see," the boy said. He took a jug of water from the night stand which his mom was trying to find. He poured water into a glass and gave it to Cera. Cera drank water while looking at the lady curiously.

"How are you feeling?" the woman asked.

"I'm feeling better, Aunty. Thank you," Cera replied.

But the boy caught Cera's attention because Cera had seen him before also. She looked at herself and saw she was wearing his hoodie and said, "Thanks for this too," He didn't say anything but "Mom, we should eat."

"Yeah, umm what is your name dear?" the lady asked.

"Oh, I'm Cera. Cera Ford."

"I'm Ella Tolger and this is my son, Jimmy Tolger. Is there anything you need, Cera?" Cera smiled warmly, grateful for the kindness of this unknown lady towards a stranger like her.

"Nothing, I'm fine thank you," Cera replied.

"Ok, then let's eat, you must be hungry," Ella said.

"Yes. but first, may I clean up? Where is the washroom?" Cera asked Jimmy. "There," he replied, pointing to the door.

.
.
.
.

COLD!

.
.
.
.

"Ok, get fresh and come. We are waiting." Ella said, Cera nodded and watched as Jimmy guided his mother out of the room. Cera smiled at them.

"Ok, Aunty."

"*Finally I found you.....*" Cera thought with a wide smile. "Well, sometimes my destiny plays from my side. Caught you, Mr. Cold!" She giggled to herself and headed to the washroom.

Chapter 5
2 WEEKS AGO

Cera parked her car and waited for him today again. It had been two days since she last saw him. She looked around leaning against her car while checking on her wristwatch from time to time.

"Where did he go? What if he left the cit—No! You need to talk to him, Cera! Yes, I'm going to do it," she was talking to herself when there hecame, making her heart flutter.

Removing her sunglasses, Cera gulped as she looked at him. His forehead was covered with his hoodie's cap and even his eyes were barely visible, but still she managed to recognize him. Her heart started to race when he was coming to his position. He put that small speaker on the ground and turned the music on.

Cera's heart skipped a beat when he took off his cap and flipped his hair. Her cheeks turned pink when he started to show his killer dance moves. Her steps started to go towards him. People surrounded him while appreciating him. Cera also went into the crowd and clapped for him. Her smile was enough to show her true feelings for him.

"How can someone be so hot and cute at the same time?" she thought, losing herself in his beauty.

After some time, he finished and bowed to everyone. He started to collect money from the audience as an appreciation in his piggy bank. Cera saw him approaching her. Her eyes slightly widened and a weird feeling overtook her.

"No....no....no....don't freak out! DON'T FREAK OUT! Act normal! Normal! Hoo!" She started to calm her racing heart.

And he was Jimmy.

He extended his hand towards Cera, asking if she enjoyed his dance and wanted to put some money in his piggy bank. Just then, she remembered she had left her purse in the car and cursed herself in her mind. She smiled awkwardly and showed her empty hands to him. Jimmy responded with a warm smile and a polite bow and was about to leave, but Cera stopped him before she lost herself again in his smile. She controlled herself.

"Wait," she called out. Hearing her, he turned again.

"I have something for you. Wait here, I'll be back," she said, hurrying towards her car while still looking at him.

Jimmy looked around as Cera ran off before he could say anything. He sighed and started to collect his stuff.

A few minutes later, when Cera returned with her purse and a huge chocolate bar, she couldn't find him there. She looked around but he was nowhere.

Disappointed, she sighed. "I didn't even get to ask him his name."

Chapter 6
Present Time

"Don't worry, Cera. Jimmy will drop you home tomorrow morning," Ella said while they were having their small late-night dinner, "Where do you live?" she continued.

Cera gulped and hesitated, looking down but again looked up after thinking something, "For now, I don't have a home," she replied with a sad chuckle.

"Oh, I'm sorry. I know it's personal, but Jimmy mentioned you were in a wedding dress...may I ask—"

"Mom, you should eat," Jimmy interrupted, knowing his mom might dig too much into Cera's history.

"It's okay," Cera said, nodding. "Actually, I ran away from my wedding because my dad was forcing me to marry someone for his own benefit."

"But dear, you should have talked to your dad. He must be worried about you," Ella said.

But Cera chuckled sadly and said, "He never worries about me, all he cares about is his wealth and prestige. That's why he was forcing me into this marriage."

Jimmy listened quietly. Cera broke the silence. "I'll leave as soon as I find a new place."

"No, no....it's fine, be comfortable here. You may stay here as long as you want, now eat well," Ella said. Jimmy looked at his mom in disbelief.

They all were eating, but the food was too spicy for Cera. She tried not to show it and continued eating, though she started hissing and sniffing.

"Cera, are you alright?" Ella asked. Jimmy also glanced at Cera and noticed her red face.

"Y-Yeah I'm fine, it's just a bit spicy," Cera said, drinking some water.

Jimmy noticed tears rolling down her cheeks and her face turning bright pink. Seeing her condition, he asked, "Are you okay?"

Ahhaaa!

Cera felt relief just from his simple concern. "Y-Yeah," she said, trying another bite but starting to cough hard. Jimmy handed her water, and she drank and calmed down a little.

"Aishh! Careful, Cera."

"Umm....I'm f-full, Aunty. Thank you so much," Cera said, though her expression was saying something else.

"Are you sure? Jimmy, give her something sweet to eat," Ella said, so Jimmy went and returned with some candies. Cera quickly took one and ate it.

"Thanks."

After sometime

"If you need anything, I'm upstairs. You can sleep in Jimmy's room, and he'll be out here. Good night." She patted Cera's head and went up to her room.

Cera stayed there and saw Jimmy was doing the dishes. "Ahem....Do you want any help?" she asked.

"No, I'm fine," he replied, without looking at her.

.

.

.

.

.

WHY SO COLD!!

.

.

.

.

.

"Jimmy, right? Ummm, do you remember we've met before also?" Cera asked, expecting some positive reply but he just looked at her with a straight face and said, "Sorry I don't remember."

"Well, I remember actu—" Cera got interrupted, "When are you leaving from here?" Jimmy asked with his expressionless tone which she found weird.

"Uh-I'll start looking for a new place tomorrow. Will you help me?" she asked hopefully again.

"No, do it by yourself and do it fast!" he said and left the kitchen without saying or listening further.

Chapter 7
Next Day

He was getting ready for work.

"Are you going to dance in the street again?" Cera asked innocently. Jimmy stopped and she added, "It seems like you don't like to talk much. By the way, you dance really well." She smiled, and he sighed as he looked at her.

"Are you going to find a place today?" he asked.

"Yeah, maybe," she replied with a small pout.

"Mom! I'm leaving," he called out to his mom before heading out for work.

"Ok, what are you going to do today?" Ella asked her son, handing him his bag.

"Didn't I tell you? I have been singing at the noon club for a few days, and later I have some food deliveries," he replied, checking his bag.

"Wow, you are a singer too!" Cera exclaimed excitedly.

"Yeah, my baby sings so well!" Ella kissed her son's cheek, making Cera giggle.

"Mom!" He wiped his cheek as he was embarrassed.

"Don't be late and be careful during work. I don't like the people in those clubs."

"Ok, Mom, bye."

"Bye," Ella said.

"Bye," Cera said.

"Huh? Aren't you coming with me?" Cera's eyes shined at Jimmy's question.

"Where?" she asked, smiling. Her smile faded when he said further, "You are going to look for a place, right?" She pouted again.

"Ok, bye, Aunty."

"Bye honey, and find a safe place and...Jimmy," Ella gulped and pulled herself to smile before saying, "T-Take care of her." Jimmy didn't respond and turned around to leave and Cera followed him.

Jimmy's house was quite far from the main city side. Cera was walking all the way behind him, being all tired as she was not habitual of walking this much.

"How long is he gonna make me walk?" she wondered while catching her breath and then he suddenly stopped and turned to her.

"Why are you still following me?" he asked, finding her still walking behind him.

"I-I don't know where to go?" she admitted, looking away.

He sighed and said a bit sternly, "Go to some residential areas and ask if they have any available places for you. Stop following me and find your own way."

"O-Ok," she said, looking around and seeing where to go, but she ended up stepping in his way again. Jimmy found it annoying.

"You there, me here!" He said, pointing in opposite directions before he started walking on his way.

Cera glared at his leaving figure. "There's no need to be so rude, mister. Well, let's pass the time," she sighed and started to walk nowhere because she was not interested in finding any new place as she wanted to stay always near to Jimmy. "I'll definitely melt your heart, Mr. Jerk!" Cera chuckled while talking to herself. She was roaming around the city feeling her freedom. She spread her arms and took a deep breath.

"Nothing to worry about. No more of Dad's scary glares or his men's poker faces. Just me and my life. I'm going to live it to the fullest, with Jimmy..." She covered her face, blushing.

People around her were giving her weird looks, but she ignored them and continued walking while looking around. Suddenly, she caught some unpleasant faces in the distance—her father's men. She immediately hid, it seemed like they were searching for her by showing other people her picture. Cera saw them coming to her direction. . Cera saw them coming in her direction. Panicked, she pressed herself against the wall, her heart racing.

She squeezed her eyes shut as they walked past her. She sighed in relief when they left. But then, she felt a hand on her shoulder, making her heart explode again. She did not dare look behind.

"Dear, could you help me carry these bags to the other side of the street?" Hearing an old voice, Cera turned around to face an elderly man and she sighed in relief. She saw he had two bags with him.

"Sure, Grandpa." She smiled and took his bags, helping him cross the street.

Chapter 8
Time skipped to evening

Cera was waiting for Jimmy at the bus stop which was on the way home because she knew he'd go from this way. Looking in the direction, she sighed while shivering in the cold weather. And then she heard grumbling in her stomach. She had not eaten anything after the sandwich she ate in the morning as she had no money.

"Yes, baby, calm down," she murmured to herself, trying to comfort her rumbling stomach. "Papa will be here soon, and then we'll go home, and I'll feed you something." She chuckled at her own silly words and she was talking to herself but someone was looking at her from a little far away, her smiling face and self-talk made him stop on his way. Cera saw him and her eyes shined again.

"Jimmy, hi." She stood up, smiling as he walked towards her.

"How was your day?" Cera asked like an ideal wife, "What are you doing here?" he asked coldly.

"Waiting for you."

"Haven't you found a place?"

"No, I looked everywhere and asked many people, but—"

"Let's go home," he said and started walking. Cera followed him gladly.

Cera and Jimmy came back home. Jimmy prepared dinner, Cera was so hungry and the food was in front of her but she was just looking at the food, thinking what if it's spicy again? Jimmy noticed her but didn't say anything. Cera gulped hard and put food in her mouth but her eyes slightly widened as it was not that spicy and she happily dug into her food.

"You should have helped her, Jimmy. She was alone. How could she find a place by herself?" Ella said.

"I had work, Mom, and it's her responsibility to find a place for herself because she left her dad and-"

"Jimmy, that's rude. You saved her and helped her. At least help her completely or there won't be any meaning to your help." Ella tried to make her son understand. Cera was just looking at them awkwardly.

"It's ok, Aunty, I know he also has work. Don't worry I'll find one soon by myself." Cera said calmly as Ella seemed worried. Jimmy stood up and walked away.

"Jimmy, I want—Jimmy?"

"He left, Aunty."

"Don't mind him, Cera. He is not usually like this, I don't know what's gotten into him." Ella said, squeezing Cera's hand.

Again the next day

"Are you serious? You refused that place because you don't like the curtains," Jimmy scoffed in disbelief. He was helping Cera find a new place, but she was rejecting those places for silly reasons which was irritating him more.

"Yeah, I don't like that color," Cera said, looking at him with a sad pout.

"What do you mean you don't like the color? And you also acted so rude and insulted that owner. If you keep acting like this, no one will offer you a place," he said, letting out a frustrated sigh.

"Hey! I get anxious if I don't find something convenient, and I also don't want—" Cera couldn't complete her sentence as Jimmy pulled her close, making her head bump on his chest.

"Can't even walk safely on the street," Jimmy said, annoyed, as he noticed a car which was about to hit Cera as she was walking a little outside the footway.

Cera was again lost in him. He was so close to her, she was just staring at his facial features—his deep brown eyes, soft pink lips, and sharp jawline. His frustrated expressions only made him more attractive to her.

"And you! Pay attention to where you're walking," he said, snapping her back to reality and moving her away.

Cera looked away, her face flushed. "I-I was—"

"Now I need to go to work. I can't waste my time with you. Go and try to find a place here," he said, handing her an address and leaving without even waiting for her reply.

Chapter 9
Time skipped to evening

Cera was again waiting for Jimmy at the same bus stop as the whole day she didn't do anything but wander around the city. That's why, she was tired and hungry, and feeling even weaker than yesterday. Her head was aching and spinning. She was not even able to sit properly, she was dozing off on the bench and then suddenly a guy approached her, noticed her condition and saw she was all alone. He sat beside her and was about to put his hand on her thigh but his hand got slapped away and that's when Cera gained consciousness.

She saw Jimmy and the other guy. "What are you doing!?" Jimmy slapped that man hard but he just managed to run away.

"Are you that stupid? He was about to do some bad things to you, how can you sleep alone on the street so carelessly? Be aware of your surroundings," Jimmy was scolding her but she was not able to respond.

"What are you doing here again? You should have gone ho—" Jimmy stopped when he saw Cera was rolling her eyes up and was about to fall but he caught her. "H-Hey? Now what's wrong with you? Wake up, Cera. Are you ok?" he asked patting her cheek but felt her heating body. He put his palm on her forehead and with a sigh, he carried her home.

At home

"W-what happened to her Jimmy," Ella asked worriedly. Jimmy placed Cera on the bed and put his Mom's hand on her head without saying anything and he went out.

"Oh my god! Jimmy, she is having such a high fever, how did—Jimmy? Jimmy?" After getting no response, she got it that he left. She also went behind him.

"I think she is not habitual to working a lot, that's why…" She still didn't get any response. "Are you making soup for her?"

"Hmm…" and that's all he replied with.

"I told you to take care of her and be with her," Ella said trying to make her son speak.

But she didn't know Jimmy was already frustrated and now he let it out on his mom, "What's wrong with you, mom? She isn't a kid, her father is a billionaire! She left him just because he was not good to her. But we are not billionaires, we have to work to fulfill our needs. And I can hardly manage for both of us."

"Calm down Jimmy, I'm just telling you to be with—"

"I'm so tired of this thing, Mom, sometimes you tell me to stay away from her because you are scared that I might do something to her while other times, you tell me to be with her, what should I do?" Ella's heart clenched hearing her son but she was trying hard to hide that. Jimmy also didn't mean to say that but all his frustration was coming out.

"I can't understand why are you even allowing her to stay with us. Mom, she has grown up in a different surrounding. She doesn't belong with us. She is doing this all drama of finding a new place, in fact, she doesn't want to leave here, but I, I can't feed her for a lifetime, because I don't have fucking money like her father does!" Jimmy sighed but continued, "Mom, I want her to leave from here as soon as possible, I don't care if she stays on the streets, because I can't let her stay here for free and pay for her food and medicines for no reason." Finally calming himself, he stopped. Ella gulped understanding her son's mental state.

"I can understand, Jimmy, I'm sorry. But just for a few days more, okay? She is alone, dear. I know you are not this harsh. I'll talk to her tomorrow." Ella hugged him while comforting him knowing it was hard for him also. But then Jimmy felt someone's presence. He saw Cera there and suddenly his words started to replay in his mind.

"I-I want some water," Cera said pretending like she didn't hear anything.

"Cera, you are up honey. How are you feeling?" Ella asked sweetly.

"I'm fine, Aunty."

"Come here, eat something. You are sick, you should have something."

"N-No, Aunty, because of fever I don't feel like eating anything. I'll just sleep," Cera said but Jimmy was looking at her swollen face with two thoughts lingering in his mind, whether she had heard everything or not.

"It's not good Cera, you shou—"

"Please, Aunty, I really don't want to," Cera's tears fell but she wiped them immediately, though Jimmy definitely noticed. She gulped looking away.

"Jimmy, I-I....I'll sleep here on the couch, you can sleep in your room. I'm not feeling well there."

"It's cold out here, in my room ther-" Jimmy said but...

"Please I'm not comfortable there," Cera said and went to the couch, Jimmy just looked at her.

After some time Ella helped Jimmy in cleaning and went to sleep. Jimmy came to look at Cera he noticed her shivering figure on the couch with not enough blankets to cover. He covered her properly and checked her temperature but even after covering her Cera was still shivering, she really had a high fever. Then he remembered the soup which he had made for her, he went to the kitchen and came back with soup and some herbal tea.

He sat near her and patted her little, "Uh, hey wake up...." Cera felt pats but she was not able to open her eyes. Cera managed to move a little, "You should drink this, your fever will be gone till the morning. Here take it, c'mon," he said helping her to sit up while cheering her little not knowing Cera was really not in her senses. He held her gently wrapping his arm around her shoulder, her head fell on his chest. Suddenly his heart started to beat faster when he felt her snuggling near his chest but still moving her hair from her face he made her drink that tea and then fed her some soup too. After she finished, he again laid her on the couch and covered her properly. He looked at her for a moment.

"I hope you will feel better soon.....I'm sorry."

He thought to himself while staring at her.

Next morning

"Jimmy, Jimmy......wake up, have you seen Cera?"

Rubbing his eyes Jimmy woke up after hearing his mom's voice. "What happened Mom?" Jimmy asked sleepily. "I'm calling Cera but she is not answering, did she go out? Did she tell you?"

Jimmy looked at her confused, "No, Mom, I didn't get to talk to her, where did she go?" They both went out to see Cera but she was nowhere in the house.

After looking around, Jimmy found a chit on the table near the couch. He opened it and read out loudly, "Dear Aunty and Jimmy, I forgot to tell you that, yesterday I found a new place, as I was sick I didn't get a chance to tell you. I needed to shift in today and you were sleeping so I didn't disturb you. Thank you so much for your love, care and kindness. Jimmy, thank you for helping me and for the soup also. I'm feeling better now. I'll always remember you guys. Bye, take care. Let's meet someday. Cera."

"I'm happy for her, I hope she is doing well. She was a nice girl, I'm gonna miss her," Ella said as she was really happy for Cera but Jimmy was thinking something else. Suddenly, it started to rain with loud thunders.

"Oh no, this rain! Jimmy, I think you should not go to work today," Ella sighed, annoyed with the continuous rain.

"No, Mom. I have to go," Jimmy said looking out of the window worriedly.

"Aishh this boy! Ok, but take care."

"Yes, Mom."

Chapter 10

Jimmy was running through the rain with his umbrella while looking for that particular face, it was hard to recognize faces because of the rain.

"Where did this girl go?"

He kept searching for Cera, he had a feeling that she lied about finding a new place because he knew that last night she had heard everything Jimmy was saying to his mom.

"Excuse me, sir? Have you seen a girl wearing a blue hoodie?" Jimmy started asking people around while explaining Cera's look but he was not able to describe her properly to them and people were also busy running to protect themselves from rain.

"No…I'm sorry," that's the only answer Jimmy was getting from people. It was raining heavily, making him worry more.

He was worried for her.

He pushed his hair back, thunders were giving him very bad vibes making his heartbeat fast. But he didn't give up.

"Where should I find you? Such a troublemaker you are!" he said, tiredly panting hard under the pouring rain and going in the other direction in her search.

And running a little further, he spotted that curled figure under the shade, covered with some kind of plastic sheets. His heart calmed down seeing her safe in front of his eyes, and a low sigh of relief left his mouth. But she was crying while covering her ears, probably scared by thunders. Jimmy ran to her, "Hey!" Cera's eyes were still squeezed closed and seemed like she didn't hear his voice.

"Cera..." he said with a small pat on her head and she looked up while still crying more. Jimmy knelt in front of her.

"So is this your new place? .....well nice choice," he said checking that plastic sheet on her. Cera wasn't saying anything as she just broke into sobs.

"Are you sure you are going to stay here? And als—" And suddenly a loud thunder cut his sentence but it hit hard on Cera's nerves and she quickly hugged him.

"No p-please, I don't want to stay here .....I-I'm scared...."

Jimmy could feel how shaky her voice was and how much she was scared. He sighed and caressed her back. "It's OK, you don't need to stay here, why did you lie?" Cera didn't say anything.

"I'm sorry...", Jimmy said holding her protectively in his arms. "I didn't mean it, I-I was frustrated because of work. You can stay with us." Jimmy still didn't get any response from her but he understood that she was just scared.

At home

"Why did you lie, Cera? Didn't I tell you not to mind him, he was a little disturbed yesterday," Ella said while drying Cera's hair. "He didn't mean it, he isn't bad, dear," Ella didn't want Cera to create any bad image about Jimmy in her mind.

"I know, Aunty, he's not bad. But I also don't want to be a burden on someone, and you are still helping me even though I'm no one to you," Cera said sadly, looking down.

"But what if something might have happened to you again....?" Cera gulped hearing her, not knowing what to say only the thought was scaring her.

"I'm sorry...." Cera could only say this. Ella sighed and said, "Don't think of yourself as a burden on us, we should help each other. That's the way to keep humanity alive. We are happy to help you."

"Ok then, I'll also find some work or any job," Cera said, holding her hand.

Jimmy came back as he had gone somewhere after dropping her home, "Here, some clothes and medicines for you, I also don't have many clothes so now don't wear mine."

"No need of medicines, I'm fine an- HaAaKk-ChHhOoo!" Jimmy rolled his eyes and went inside. Ella chuckled, "Go get changed then we'll eat together." Cera nodded and left.

Time skipped

The whole day Cera didn't get to talk with Jimmy as he was busy but she had a good time with his mom as Cera knew Ella was really a very kind lady.

Jimmy was standing alone, having his own time when Cera came.

"Jimmy....?" He turned to her. "I-I made coffee for you," Cera said while handing him the coffee mug, he didn't say anything just looked at her baggy clothes which he had bought for her, some oversized tee and loose shorts. He didn't notice her wearing those until now.

Cera noticed him looking at her and looked at herself and he looked away and said, "I didn't know what you wear so I just got what I like," Cera smiled, "It's ok, I like it, it's really comfortable. Thank you." They both sipped on coffee.

Silence......

"I'm sorry...." he spoke.

"It's ok, I can understand." She turned to him, "Yeah, it was my stupidity to leave my father, but I really don't want to go back there again. That was more than a hell for me and I always felt caged there, in my own house. There was no one even to care if I died in that cage."

He was listening to her. She chuckled sadly. "I'm sorry, I didn't mean to bother you. I just found an escape here and finally was able to breathe and definitely liked it. I thought I was free now, forgetting that I'm dependent on someone."

"I really didn't mean," he managed to utter as he was a little guilty. He was not the type of person who hurt someone with words like that. He was very warm-hearted and sensitive.

Cera put her coffee mug aside and removed something from her neck, it was a pendant which was the only thing she was wearing all this time. She showed it to him.

"It's a real diamond, my mom gave it to me," she said and held his hand, putting it on his palm. He looked at her confused and she continued, "For now, I don't have anything to give you except this, but you'll get money if you—"

"What are you saying? I don't want this, I'm no—" he refused to take it. "I really don't want to be a burden on someone," she said again, closing his fist.

"Cera, I told you that I really didn't mean to say it. Mom also won't like it so jus-"

"Jimmy, please keep it."

He paused, seeing her glittering eyes in the moonlight, and sighed. He couldn't say much. She left from there, he looked at her and then at her pendant.

Chapter 11

"For Mom.... hmm," she read on that piggy bank-like thing which Jimmy had with him when he was collecting money after dancing on the street. She smiled as she looked at him sleeping peacefully on the bed.

Since Cera had been sleeping on the couch—she was comfortable there—Jimmy was sleeping in his own room. Cera was here to take a shower and was about to go inside the bathroom but this small thing caught her attention, she pressed her lips sadly, "I wish I could help you." She looked at it for a while before going to the washroom.

After taking a shower, Cera realized that she didn't bring her clothes and Jimmy was sleeping out. She whined, annoyed at herself, and wrapped the towel around her body before she slightly opened the door and peeped out. She saw Jimmy was still fast asleep, so she sighed and went out.

Meanwhile

Jimmy slowly opened his eyes but those went wide, his cheeks heated up when he saw Cera near the bathroom door while she was adjusting her towel around herself. He quickly closed his eyes.

Cera once again looked at Jimmy and he was still sleeping so she slowly went to get her clothes without making any sound and after grabbing her clothes just like that she again went inside the bathroom.

Jimmy sighed, hearing the sound of the closing door, he sat up and put his hand on his chest to feel his abnormally beating heart. He gulped and looked at the bathroom and suddenly......

"Good morning," Cera said coming out of the bathroom wearing her clothes, with a bright smile on her face.

"G-Good morning," he replied and suddenly ran out of the room. She gave him a confused look but shrugged.

"Huh- what's wrong with him?" she thought, but shook her head and continued drying her hair.

"Aunty... are you cooking?" Cera entered the kitchen and saw Ella cooking.

"Umm.... yeah sometimes I try and it turns out good," Ella chucked.

"Ok I'll also help you," Cera said taking some veggies to cut.

"Do you know how to cook?" Ella asked.

"Not really but I can bake well, I can make you cake," Cera said while looking around the ingredients, "Oh yeah, I can make a cake, we also have some ingredients!" She said again looking around for the ingredients.

"Haha....A-Are you sure, Cera?" Ella asked with a nervous laugh.

"Don't worry, Aunty. I know how to bake a cake, well, that's the only thing I can make.... hehe," Cera replied while collecting the ingredients.

"Okey.....?" Ella moved a little aside when Cera started her work.

After a few minutes

"And now sugar...." Cera took the sugar. But don't know why Ella touched it to check and gasped.

"Oh, no Cera! It's not sugar, it's salt!" Cera's eyes widened hearing Ella and she immediately put that aside.

"Oh my—thank you, aunty. You are so sharp." Hearing Cera's worried tone, Ella laughed. Cera was so amazed that Ella couldn't see but was so accurate about things no wonder how she managed to cook.

"What's going on here?" Their giggles stopped when they heard Jimmy.

"We are making a cake," Cera said showing him the batter.

"Why?" he asked curiously.

"For you....." Cera replied fondly smiling at him. His mom chuckled.

"Yeah, she wanted to make one. I don't know how to bake, so you'll also have some homemade cake," Ella said.

"But we don't have a microwave," he told Cera.

"It's ok, I never make cake in a microwave. I'm afraid of microwaves, so I can bake it in my way," she winked at him, making him suddenly flustered.

"Aren't you going to work today?" Ella asked Jimmy.

"No, actually the club is closed today .... I'll go, but late," he replied.

"Fine, you can rest at least," she said and they all heard a knock on the main door.

"I'll check," Jimmy said and went to check.

As soon as Jimmy opened the door, a huge smile made its way to his lips.

"JIMMY!" A boy around the same age as Jimmy pulled him in a hug, and Jimmy gladly hugged him back.

Meanwhile, Cera and Ella were still in the kitchen but suddenly some chaos was heard by them. Cera heard a familiar voice.

"Mom, Jack is here!" Jimmy yelled from outside.

"Jack?" Cera's eyes widened upon hearing the name, and they both went out.

And as soon as Jack saw Cera, "Cera....?" He was so surprised that he went straight to her and hugged her closing his eyes in relief.

"Where were you? I searched for you everywhere.... I was so worried. How are you? I had told you to come straight to my house after running from there, hadn't I? Then—" Jack stopped as Cera was just looking at him waiting for him to calm down. Jimmy and his mom seemed confused.

"I'm fine Jack, thanks to Jimmy...." Cera said with a small smile to assure him and continued, "Yeah, you had told me to come to your house but I knew dad would first go to search me there so I skipped that plan."

But then she saw his teary eyes, "Hey! Why are you crying? I'm fine Jack."

"Cera, we almost searched everywhere, I was......I was scared. I thought I lost you. That's why we were here to ask Jimmy for help but—"

"We? Who is with you?" Cera interrupted him, Jack sighed knowing Cera would not like the idea of him bringing the person here with him. And that's what happened the person entered and Cera's eyes widened. She shifted herself behind Jack.

But Jimmy seemed happy seeing the person after so long.

"Hey, Harold!" Jimmy went to him and helped him with his umbrella and then turning to each other, they hugged, Harold smiled until his eyes fell on Cera.

"C-Cera....? W-What are you—" Harold was about to go to her but she stepped back hugging Jack's arm, he sighed "Ok I'm sorry, you know I can't go against your dad."

Harold was her dad's special person, who was more like a son to her dad, who her dad trusted the most. Harold was someone more important to her Dad than she was.

Jack didn't know what to say as Cera was hiding behind him, "Calm down," he assured Cera.

"Then why did you bring him here with you?" She slapped Jack's shoulder, her voice cracking as tears were filling in her eyes.

"Cera, I was scared. I had no option, only Harold could have helped me with this," Jack said trying to explain the situation.

"I don't wanna come with you!" Cera said to Harold trying to make it clear but tears were already falling from her eyes.

Jimmy noticed how scared Cera was.

"Don't be stubborn, Cera," Harold said trying to make her understand but...

"No! I won't go back there, please....Jack, say something." She started to cry.

"Ok, ok, don't cry, no need to be this scared, okay?" Jack said, trying to comfort her, and wiped her tears.

"Your dad is finding you, he is going crazy, Cera. He wants you in front of him right now." Harold was trying hard to tell her the seriousness of the situation but Cera didn't want to understand anything.

"Then tell him I died," Cera yelled frustratedly.

"Oh no, Cera, don't say like this dear..." Ella said trying to find her, so Cera quickly hugged her.

"Aunty, I don't wanna go back there again." Cera cried, hugging her tight.

"Fine, don't go. Harold, please let her stay with us and don't tell her father anything about it." Ella said as she was worried about Cera and didn't want to force her for anything.

"But Aunty, you don't know her father. Even if I don't tell him anything, he'll find her anyhow." Harold was just trying to make the situation light by taking everything straight but he was not understanding the fact Cera was not ready to go back there.

Harold was not a bad guy, he was like an older brother to Cera. But he always stayed under the command of Cera's dad.

"I know, Harold but you should think about her also," Ella said, caressing Cera to calm her. Harold thought something and sighed.

"Ok fine, stay here. I won't tell your dad," Harold said. Cera looked at him wiping her tears.

"I don't believe you," Cera madly purred at him, he chuckled.

"Ayyee, come here. And believe me," he said, pulling her in a hug. "I was worried, you should have told me also that you were going to run away." He pecked her forehead.

"So you could destroy every chance for me to run away?" Cera said coldly moving away from him but he laughed.

Chapter 12

"Oh my mommy! I missed you," Jack whined like a baby as he clung to Ella.

"Oh my baby, I missed you too." She put her hand on his face and kissed his cheek.

"Will anyone bother to tell me what's happening here?" They heard Jimmy's voice who was silent all this time.

"And please tell me too, how you ended up here," Harold asked while taking a seat. And everyone sat there to clear all confusion.

Jack Pros was Jimmy's best friend. When Jimmy was new and alone in the city, Jack was the one who always helped him. And with that, they became good friends and grew closer to each other.

And about Cera and Jack, they were buddies from middle school and he was the only friend Cera had for now because Jack was close enough to Harold also. And through Jack, Harold came to know about Jimmy.

Jack and Harold always came to meet Jimmy and Ella. As Jimmy never liked to get along with new people, Jack also never mentioned him much to her people. But once while talking accidentally, Jack spilled about Jimmy to Harold, though not in a bad way. He was just giving an example of a hard-working guy and he could think of none other than Jimmy. And that's when Harold wanted to meet Jimmy because he had started to admire him just by hearing about him. And one day he met Jimmy. Harold adored Jimmy for his unique personality and became friends with him.

But in all these things, surprisingly Jimmy and Cera were unaware of each other. Jack also never brought Jimmy's topic or name to Cera to protect Jimmy's privacy.

Well, the world is small.

And here, the two were living under the same roof.

After hearing everything from Cera and Jimmy about how Cera ended up here with Jimmy, Harold said, "Thank you so much, Jimmy, please let her stay here. Her father doesn't care about her but I do."

Jimmy was already so happy seeing Harold and Jack after so long. They were his only friends, Cera could sense that happiness in his eyes. She never saw Jimmy smiling like that.

"Sure, Harold. She can stay here with us," Jimmy assured Harold.

Cera was staring at Jimmy while smiling fondly and her friend Jack noticed it.

"What smell is th- OH MY GOD!! Cera, the CAKE!!" Ella exclaimed realizing what smell it was. "OH NO!" Cera ran into the kitchen followed by Jack.

Cera sighed in relief after seeing her cake all fine, just a few layers were burnt. She continued to fix her cake while glancing out at Jimmy who was talking with Harold. Jack was looking at her every action and when she caught him looking at her, he just gave her a teasing smirk.

"What?" she asked.

"You know what, he is the best!" he replied with a smile. She chuckled and said, "I know."

"Woahh! Your story seems so like a movie, like you were in danger and he came to save you, he fought for you and protected you and then you fell in love with him," he said dramatically and she looked at him, surprised.

"How do you know that I like him?" she asked, he just ruffled her hair.

"It's in your eyes," he said and she smiled.

"You know, I liked him even before that," she said, now surprising him.

"Really?"

"That boy I told you about who dances on the street, that's him!" she said and his eyes shined.

"Are you serious? So cool!" he said giving her a high-five.

"He is so kind, sometimes acts like a jerk but from inside he is very soft, caring and ….lovely." She was lost in her thoughts with dreams in her eyes while talking about Jimmy.

Jack smiled. "He also needs someone like you," he said making her snap back. She looked at him confused and he continued, "His life isn't easy, Cera. He is broken….He is shattered. He deserves someone's genuine trust and love." Cera was not understanding anything but she smiled as he was smiling.

"What do you mean?" she asked curiously.

"He'll tell you himself once he gets comfortable with you. He is very innocent, he is a pure soul. People took advantage of his innocence, used him and broke him at a very young age. Don't break him or his trust ever …." he said, Cera could see a kind of worry in his eyes. She gulped before speaking, "I'll never hurt him, I'll never leave him."

Jack flicked her forehead and said, "First confess to him about your feelings you dumbo!"

"I don't know how to, he acts so coldly towards me. And first I want to help him, I don't want to be a burden on him. Will you help me to find a job?"

Jack looked at her little surprised after hearing her, "You wanna do a job? ... I mean it's good but if you start working, your dad will find you easily. It's not a good idea," Cera just hummed in response.

"Ok, taste it," she said, feeding Jack a small piece of cake.

"Ahem." Someone interrupted them and again a teasing smirk appeared on Jack's lips.

"Nothing bro.... nothing. It's not what you are thinking. We are just friends. Just friends!" He said dramatically. Jimmy gave him a weird look but he got a hard stomp on his foot by Cera, "Ahhh!" He looked at her in disbelief.

"What's wrong with you?" Jimmy asked finding his friend's actions strange.

"I-I.... I mean.....WAHH!! WHAT a cake! Come here," Jack said pulling Jimmy to stand beside him.

"Cera, feed him," Jack said and Cera gladly took a piece of cake and before Jimmy could say anything she shoved it in his mouth.

"What th-" Jimmy stopped mid-sentence because the taste of cake melted in his mouth.

"How is it?" Cera asked.

"It's.....nice," Jimmy said, a little surprised because the cake was really tasty.

"Ok then, it's done! Cera's going to open a cake shop," Jack announces out of the blue, even shocking Cera herself along with Jimmy.

"W-What?" Cera was clueless.

"Good idea," Harold said coming inside the kitchen with Ella.

"Well, I agree, if Cera wants to do it," Ella said while tasting the cake.

"We will help you. Wooo!!" Jack said, hyping Cera. Cera smiled and looked at Jimmy and asked, "Will you?" Jimmy gave her a little smile for the first time, causing her heart to flutter, and nodded.

"But do we need a place?" Jimmy asked.

"No, I guess, we'll take orders from home first, then according to our earnings we will look for a place. What do you say?" Cera said making her own plans but they agreed.

"Smart! I'm impressed!" Jack clapped for her.

After sometime

After discussing her new business idea, Jack and Harold were ready to leave.

"Here is some money to start something new," Harold said, handing Cera money.

"No. I don't want anything from him. It's his money, my beginning will be cursed," Cera said giving the money back to him.

"Don't be stubborn again. You will need this." Harold tried to convince her but, "No, I'll go with a loan," Cera replied. Harold sighed and was about to hand the money to Jack but Cera glared at Jack telling him not to take so he just put his hands up in the air. Harold didn't offer it to Jimmy knowing he'll never accept.

"Ok, good luck!" Harold kept the money back and patted Cera's cheek.

Jack and Harold turned to leave.

"Harold," Cera called out, and he again turned to her. "Don't tell him please," she said with pleading eyes.

"Don't worry. I won't tell him. Take care," Harold patted her head to assure her.

"Bye, Mommy. Take care, I'll come back soon," Jack said, again clinging to Ella.

"Yes, and you too. Come back soon. Bye," Ella said, hugging him.

And after bidding their goodbyes, they left.

Chapter 13
Next Day

He closed his eyes to feel the voice of the person who was singing in front of him. That's the voice he was looking for. Jimmy's voice was so angelic, he was so lost in that music that he only snapped back when Jimmy stopped singing. He opened his eyes and saw Jimmy was bowing and thanking everyone as they were giving him applause. He also started to clap for Jimmy.

Jimmy's work time was over, his boss came to give him his today's earnings.

"Boss, may I have some more today? I need it. I'll overwork someday for this," Jimmy asked his boss for some more money. His boss didn't say much and gave him some extra money because he also knew how honest Jimmy was. "Thank you so much," Jimmy thanked his boss and turned to leave but then……

"Hi, Jimmy…..?" An unknown guy approached Jimmy.

"Yes…Hello," Jimmy said looking at him as he looked a little familiar.

"I'm Mike Carter, also known as—"

"Mikey C! Oh- I know you, sir," Jimmy cut him mid-sentence. Mike smiled seeing Jimmy's shining eyes and he extended his hand for a shake and Jimmy gladly accepted. Jimmy seemed surprised but he was so happy.

"I'm a huge fan of your rapping sir, I watch all your videos." Jimmy was excited.

"Haha, thank you," Mike bowed slightly.

"But how do you know me?" Jimmy asked curiously.

"Jack... Jack Pros, He told me about you, and really you sing so well. Fabulous! Your voice is so angelic Jimmy," Mike said praising his voice.

"Thank you, sir," Jimmy said, a little nervous as someone after a long time praised him genuinely like this.

"I want to talk to you... can we?" Mike asked, only if he was comfortable.

"Sure, sir."

"Hey, don't call me sir. I'm not a greater artist than you, you can call me Mike," Mike said to make Jimmy comfortable with him.

"Ok s— Mike," Jimmy corrected himself and Mike smiled patting his shoulder.

"So, what do you want to talk about?" Jimmy asked.

"Not here, let's talk somewhere else?"

Jimmy nodded and they both left from there.

Mike and Jimmy went to some café to talk.

"Jimmy if you know, I release my albums under the SGT company. And our company wants to form a New Boy Band under my lead and also launch new solo artists. I asked Jack too and he suggested me to meet you as he said you are also a good singer and dancer as well. So, would you like to give it a try? I mean would you like to give an audition for this?" Mike explained things to Jimmy but Jimmy gulped and looked at him for a moment.

"Umm, thank you, Mike, for offering me this but I'm s-sorry. I'm r-really not i-interested," Jimmy said, forcing a small smile, trying not to sound rude.

"What? I mean, are you serious? I'm- wait- are you nervous about the selection? Don't worry about that Jimmy, for me you are already selected. You need to give an audition just for formality. Trust me, you are so talented and we need someone like you, your voice in our group. You'll be our star, Jimmy," Mike said trying to convince Jimmy. Jimmy started to think something.

"See if yo- umm excuse me," Mike excused himself to answer his phone.

Jimmy was slowly losing himself in overthinking.

He was drowning in his own thoughts.

After a few minutes, Mike turned to Jimmy again after hanging up and said, "Don't make quick decisions, Jimmy, because you can do many things. Think again. This is my card, call me if you change your mind, ok?" Mike gave Jimmy his card. "I need to leave for now but think twice and don't forget that you are amazing! Hope to see you soon," Mike said and Jimmy did a slight bow thanking him as he was ready to leave and Mike left from there. Jimmy looked at his card and then at his figure walking away from him and sighed.

After sometime

"Are you dumb? Do you know who he is? And you just rejected his offer.....I can't believe!" Jack was so in disbelief.

"Jack, you know why I rejected," Jimmy replied followed by a moment of silence on the phone, but he continued "Yeah I'm scared."

"How long, Jimmy? How long are you going to live like this? Your life is giving you a chance, think wise... if you make it, you can give a better life to your mom, and you can also achieve your dreams," Jack said trying to convince his friend.

"Jack, why don't you understand? I can—"

"Why don't *you* understand, Jimmy? Please think again," Jack said again, interrupting Jimmy.

"Jimmy! I got my first orders!" Cera came inside interrupting both of them who were talking on the phone. She was so happy and started to run around Jimmy.

"Yeayyyy! Cera got her first order." Hearing Cera, Jack also said loudly through the phone, making Jimmy move his phone away from his ear.

"Hey!! You two! Don't scream!" Jimmy said getting annoyed with their chaos. But again he said, "Nice! you got your first order, so congratulations!.... and Jack I'll call you lat—"

"Wait, is this Jack? I wanna talk," Cera said, taking the phone from Jimmy.

Jack congratulated Cera and they had their buddy chit-chat for a few minutes and then they hung up. Then she turned to Jimmy and gave him his phone back and continued smiling at him. Jimmy noticed, looking away he went to the cupboard to get something and when he returned to Cera, she was still smiling at him.

"W-Why are you s-smiling like that? It's weird." Hearing him, she chuckled.

"Because I like you," Cera replied, still with that bright smile, but he looked away pretending he didn't hear it.

"This is some money if you need.... no need to get a loan. For the beginning, it would be enough," he said, giving Cera an envelope. She looked at it and again at him.

He noticed her hesitation and said, "Do you remember, you gave me your pendant?"

Her smile started to fade, hearing him.

"That's it. This is your money, not mine so take it." He handed her the money. She felt a little bad. "Thanks..." she said, forcing a small smile. He nodded and turned to leave....

"Jimmy, I said, I like you," Cera said again as he had just ignored her earlier confession.

He stopped, "Don't," he said without turning to her and left from there.

Cera pouted sadly but, "C'mon Cera, get to work." She cheered herself up and also left the room.

Chapter 14
After Two Months

"6...7...8...9 and 10," Cera counted, putting the boxes of cake on one another, ready to deliver.

Cera was getting pretty good orders for cake, people were liking her cakes and also she was earning well so she decided to start her business in a shop.

"Cera, I'll deliver these 4 to Park Lumos Hotel and you take these to BBM school, ok?" Jack said as he was also there to help her with deliveries, "And Jimmy, have you talked to that shop owner, is he ready to give his shop on rent?"

"Yeah, they said we can take their place from next week," Jimmy said, tying his shoelace and picking some boxes to help Cera.

"Okeyyy! We'll open the shop!!" Cera said, clapping excitedly.

"Yeah but stop overworking, you have been getting sick lately. You are not habituated to working a lot dear," Ella said.

"No, Mom, I'm getting habituated now. I'm not overworking, I'm enjoying working," Cera said, hugging Ella from the side.

Mom. Yeah, that's what Cera called Ella. In these few months, Cera was sharing a special bond with each of them. Those strangers have become her family or more than family. Cera asked Ella if she could call her Mom, and Ella gladly allowed.

Cera had lost her mom at a very young age and since then, she'd never felt that motherly affection from anyone else until now when

Ella was giving her all love and affection, treating her like her own daughter.

"Ok, Mom, we are leaving," Jimmy said, as they all became ready to go.

"Ok, bye, take care."

On the way

"Jimmy, what have you thought?" Cera asked while walking.

"Or are you still thinking? It's been so long...." Jack also asked, accompanying her.

"Yeah..." Cera turned to Jimmy and Jimmy stopped, and so did they. Jimmy was so confused.

"What are you guys talking about?" Jimmy asked both of them. But Cera and Jack looked at each other, confused.

"Cera, I think, we both are talking about different things." Hearing Jack, Cera thought something.

"Yeah, I guess, never mind," Cera said and continued walking, followed by both the boys.

Jack was talking about Mike's offer to Jimmy for an audition, while Cera was talking about that confession to Jimmy who hadn't seemed to change his mind about it.

Time skipped to evening

"Mom, please just for a few days," Jack was begging in front of Ella for something.

"No, I don't stay without Mom even for a single day. I won't let her go," Jimmy said interrupting.

LET ME HEAL YOU

"What are you? A kid? C'mon, Jimmy, Mom will enjoy it there," Jack tried to convince Jimmy but.....

"No Jack, I also never go out like this. I feel uncomfortable and I also never leave Jimmy—" Ella was denying...

"It's not like Jimmy will be all alone here, Cera will be with him," Jack said, suddenly making Cera choke on the air but he continued.

"Mom, you call me your son, right? Then why are you being partial? Yeah, Jimmy is your real son, why would yo—" Jack said, being dramatic.

"No Jack, I didn't mean that. I just do- ok fine," Ella agreed, falling for Jack's drama and started roaming her hands in the air to find Jack and he quickly held her hand, putting it on his cheek.

"Yeayy! It means you'll come with me?" Jack again asked to confirm.

"Yes, I will."

"Yesss! Just for a few days. Trust me you'll like it there. There will be other ladies too, so you won't be bored. Just my Boss wants to see our moms and he has some fun plans for them all," Jack said excitedly, but Jimmy seemed worried.

"What do you mean for your boss? Can't you tell him-"

But before Jimmy completed...

"Tell him that I don't have a mom?" Jack said, making a sad tone.

"Jimmy, don't be so mean, ok?" Ella said caressing Jack. "No baby, I'll come with you. Don't mind him."

Jimmy sighed seeing Jack's drama, but Jack winked at Cera, she didn't get it at first but her eyes widened realizing it.

"And don't worry about Jimmy, Cera will take good care of him, right Cera?" Jack's teasing was making Cera flustered.

"Y-Yeah..." she managed to utter and looked at Jimmy but quickly looked away.

After sometime

Jack and Ella were ready to leave but .....

"Jimmy?" Ella was hesitating to say something. Jimmy held her hand and she hugged him and said, "Jimmy, you know what I always worry about, so take care." Jimmy got it, sometimes it broke his heart but now it had become his habit so he didn't mind.

"Yes, Mom."

They moved away from each other. With that, Jack and Ella left from there. Jimmy sighed and turned around and saw Cera. They both looked at each other and then looked away awkwardly. From now on, they were going to be alone in the house.

Cera came back to the kitchen to check on her cakes and got busy at work.

But while working, suddenly....

"No! No! Ahk- No!" Cera yelped in pain shaking her hand, and the small container fell from her hand. She had accidentally burnt her hand.

Jimmy rushed to the kitchen, hearing Cera's scream.

"Cera? Wh-" He saw that flour was all over the floor and there she was in pain while holding her hand.

"What happened? Are you ok?" he asked going near her and gently holding her hand.

"It burnt a little, it's ok," she said but he noticed that her fingers were swelled.

"It's not little, Cera, you have burnt all of your fingers," he said looking at her hand, but her eyes were on his hand which was holding hers so gently and carefully, not to hurt her more. But suddenly, he dragged her out of the kitchen.

"Can't you be a bit careful? You are so clumsy," he said, carefully treating her. But she didn't say anything as she was busy staring at him. "Is there anything that you can do without making any trouble?"

"Yeah," she replied without taking her eyes off him.

"What?"

"Stare at you."

He stopped and looked up at her and saw she was really staring at him.

"Your eyes are so beautiful, Jimmy," she said, looking into his eyes.

"What about now?" he asked, suddenly crisscrossing his eyes weirdly, catching her off guard with his sudden funny action. And seeing her reaction, he started to laugh, she blinked a few times and chuckled.

"Haha…you are funny too," she laughed along with him and now he started to get lost in her smile but he looked away, calming his suddenly racing heart.

"Don't work in the kitchen, if it's not urgent order. Take some rest," he said as he completed bandaging her hand and she nodded.

Cera was continuously trying on Jimmy to get his reaction. She was trying hard to know what was in his heart for her. Why he was always ignoring her confessions and avoiding her without giving any reason? Now, Jimmy was not so cold with Cera as he had started to trust and she had become family to them but also he was that close with her. And on the other hand, Cera was falling for him more and more.

Chapter 15

AFTER 2 DAYS

"Cera? Cera!...Cera!.... where is she?" Jimmy was searching for Cera as she had received some new cake orders. But Cera was nowhere to be found in the house.

It was drizzling outside, he went out to look but his heart fluttered again seeing the view in front of his eyes. He let out a calm breath when his heart started to increase its pace.

There was Cera, sitting near the pond and sending paper boats. Jimmy slowly started to step towards her while unconsciously adoring her every small action. Cera was smiling and sometimes pouting when her boat was sinking in water and she was clapping and praising herself when the boat was floating on water. A small smile formed on his lips, this wasn't the first time he got this ticklish feeling. Whenever he was around her, his heart always acted like this, but he tried to control these feelings and kept to himself for some reason.

Cera saw Jimmy. "Jimmy... see my boats. All are drowned but thank God! These two survived," she was talking but he was just looking at her.

That slow-motion thing was happening, he could see her lips were moving slowly, but it was like he was not hearing anything but lost in those cute expressions she was making while talking.

"Take this and make yours, do you know how to make a paper boat?" she said handing him a paper.

And he snapped back.

"Uh- no," he said unconsciously, even though he knew how to do it.

"Ok, I'll teach you. First, take paper and...." She started to explain to him but here again, he was not listening to her but was just getting lost in her.

"Ta-Daa!"

He again snapped back and saw that paper boat in her hand.

"N-Nice," he smiled a little.

"Let's send these in water," she said moving a little forward and putting those boats in water. She started to give waves to water with her hand.

Cera was so fascinated with those moving boats "Wow! Jimmy, see it's movin- ahh!" Accidentally her foot slipped and she was about to fall into the water, but she felt a tight hug from behind, saving her.

She slowly started to open her squeezed eyes feeling him so close. His warm breath was striking on her neck giving her whole zoo inside her stomach. His hands were firmly holding on her waist. Her back was pressed against his chest.

And then she heard his voice echo in her ear, "Careful."

He pulled her back and they both stood straight and to break that awkward silence, she said, "Isn't it cute?"

They both sat there as the rain had stopped, they were looking at those boats silently, and then she turned to him.

"Jimmy, umm.... Jack told me about that audition thing, why don't you try?"

Jimmy looked at her as she asked out of the blue but with a light sigh he said, "I'm not interested."

"Are you sure? I mean, if you don't have any problem singing in the club, then what's wrong with singing as an artist? And you will earn well." Cera was hesitating to talk about it but she had to do it as Jack had asked her to do so.

"I .... I don't want to," he said, looking away.

Cera gulped, trying to understand him and decided not to stretch the topic much, "By the way, I have never heard you singing.... So—" She stopped when he looked at her, "It's ok, haha," she laughed nervously.

But.....

"More you try to go away from me,
I'll make you feel loved that more....."
"More you try to break yourself,
I'll make you fix yourself that more....."
"More you try to hurt me,
I'll make you love me that more......"
"Try to kill my love more and more......more and more
I'll still love you like sea loves the shore....."

He was singing, his eyes were closed and she was looking at him. Admiring him with her whole heart. His voice was beautiful and calming with the low sound of flowing water. He slowly started to move with the rhythm.

He was so attractive.

Mesmerizing....

But he stopped singing and opened his eyes to see her completely lost in his eyes. She was not even blinking. Jimmy blinked and looked away.

"Jimmy....."

He again looked at her, and she came closer to him, putting her hand gently on his cheek, she caressed it. They were looking into each other's eyes as if they were trying to say something or ask something.

LET ME HEAL YOU

She slowly started to lean in and he closed his eyes and felt her lips on his. She slowly pressed and moved her lips against his, and so did he.

He was feeling it....

So much care....

So much passion....

So much LOVE....

But suddenly Jimmy shot open his eyes and stood up. Cera flinched and opened her eyes.

"Jimmy?"

She also stood up.

"W-What are you d-doing?" He was about to leave from there but she held his arm. But he didn't turn to her.

"I love you, Jimmy," she said and he looked at her. "I love you, you're very special to me. You mean a lot to me." Tears filled her eyes, not wanting to get any heartbreak.

He was not saying anything.

"Jimmy, I-I'm not forcing yo—" she couldn't complete and sobbed looking down as she was not so good at putting her feelings in words. Jimmy was not saying anything but continued looking at her while thinking something.

He cupped her face and made her look at him. "Hey, why are you crying?" He asked, wiping her tears.

She blinked, looking at him. He gave her a small smile, "Do you really love me?"

She nodded, sniffing cutely.

"Then let's go," he said, holding her wrist, and dragging her inside the house.

"Jimmy what are yo-" Before she completed, she was pinned to the door by him. He smirked.

"C'mon, babe, show me how much you love me," he said and started to kiss her roughly.

Cera felt a little strange. She moved him a little but he grabbed her hands and pinned them up over her head and started to plant kisses on her neck too. Her heart was beating and banging in her chest, she was having mixed weird feelings. He was going so rough like he was not Jimmy but....

Someone else....

"Jimmy, s-stop. It h-hurts."

"It's ok, sweetheart." He picked her up and threw her on the bed.

Cera gulped when he removed his shirt and threw it away.

"Do you want me to remove your clothes, darling?" He said slowly walking towards her. Cera started to move back on the bed.

She was scared....

Those flashbacks from the night when Jimmy had saved her from those bad guys, but now Jimmy was also sounding like them.

"J-Jimmy, w-what are you d-doing?"

Chapter 16

Jimmy was walking closer towards Cera. He was scary.

"Ahk—"

He harshly pushed her on the bed and hovered over her. Tears started to flow from her eyes.

"You love me, right? Then show me....c'mon," he said and pinned both her hands on the bed.

"Jimmy, you are hurting me." She broke into sobs.

"Shuu! It happens. Why are you crying? You love me, can't you do this for me?"

Cera was feeling suffocated, she was crying hard. She didn't know why he was acting like that. She was not able to do anything else but cry.

"I l-love you Jimmy, b-but please s-stop..... I'm scared." She cried helplessly closing her eyes. Jimmy was looking at her desperation blankly.

Seeing her crying like that was definitely breaking his heart but still, he was doing it on purpose. He released her and moved back but she still stayed like that while crying even harder.

"You love me, then why are you scared to give yourself to me? Is this the way you love me?"

Cera opened her eyes and looked at him confused. She knew he was not like this but she didn't know what made him act this way or what he was trying to prove.

"What? N-no Jimmy, I-I Ahk—" she yelped in pain holding her neck. Jimmy quickly helped her. He had harshly pushed her onto the bed, her neck was hurt a little. But she saw his tears fall, and he looked away.

"No Jimmy, I really love y-you. It's j-just you suddenly changed l-like that, it caught me so off guard, so I was just scared. I know y-you won't hurt m-me, I can do a-anything for you," she desperately held his hand.

"You can't even take this much pain or any harsh treatment, Cera. Your whole life will be painful after knowing me completely. You will only get hurt if you try to stand with me. Love? There's noth—"

"I love you... I-I can take any p-pain for you, trust m-me," she was not able to stop crying, not knowing how to prove him.

Jimmy was just looking at her, the way she was trying hard to convince him of how much she loved him.

"Ok fine, let's do whatever you want. I'm ready," she said, moving Jimmy on the bed and sitting on his lap.

"C-Cera...."

She started to remove her top, Jimmy looked away.

"Cera, d-don't."

"Let's do it. If this is the way you'll believe my love then, fine."

"Stop it, Cera!" He held her hands to stop her.

"No, Jimmy, please let me prove my love. I don't have words to tell you how much I love you and what you mean to me," she was crying hysterically.

Jimmy slowly hugged her and started to cry, "I'm sorry."

"When I first saw you, I just fell in love with your looks. It was love at first sight. But here, after living with you I can't stop myself from falling for the real you." She was confessing everything and he was just listening to her without saying anything.

"I want you to be someone special in my life, who'll walk with me till the end. I want to give you my everything because now I only have you." She felt him hugging her tight.

"Don't try to push me away, Jimmy."

"I'm sorry," he said hugging her tighter like he wanted to hide somewhere inside of her. She kissed his head and let him cry on her chest.

"You don't know a-anything about m-me, Cera. P-People say I'm n-not a good person, even my m-mom doesn't t-trust me. If y-you stand w-with me, they w-will hurt y-you too."

Cera was taken aback by his words, she was confused. His voice was shaky.

"I-I don't w-want you to get h-hurt because of m-me, I'm t-trying top-protect you, Cera."

Cera moved back and cupped his face to take a look at him. His eyes watered and he looked scared.

"I don't care, Jimmy, whatever people say about you. I'm always standing by you no matter what. Trust me."

He was still crying but she felt like something else was hurting him more. "What happened?" she said, wiping his tears.

Jimmy paused and looked at her. He moved her aside from his lap and she started to wear her top. He avoided looking at her as he was ashamed of his behavior. Cera was waiting for him to say something but he was not saying anything. So she again held his face and made him look at her. He saw his marks on her neck which only made him feel guiltier. He gently touched her neck.

"I'm sorry Cera, I really couldn't understand you. I-I thought.... I thoug—"

"That I'm being childish and my love would last just 4 days and will vanish soon, like a teenage girl having a crush."

He looked at her and nodded hesitantly.

"You'll leave me in the middle when you will know about me completely and my pas—" He closed his eyes mid-sentence and tears again started to fall from his eyes.

"No Jimmy, why are you thinking like that? Please trust me, try to understand me," she said holding his hands.

He again looked up at her, his eyes were saying so many things but he was not sure if he should trust someone again or not.

"I-I'm scared, Cera, I don't want to get hurt again. It h-hurts so much, please don't hurt me ever," his hands were shaking, and he was crying like he was suffering from some kind of trauma. But she pecked his lips and wiped his tears.

"I'll never." She hugged him and caressed his back to calm him down.

After sometime

Standing on the balcony, they were feeling evening breezes. Jimmy had been staring at Cera for a long time so she looked away, feeling her cheeks heating up. She hugged his arm and rested her head on his shoulder, "Why are looking at me like that?"

"Were you scared?" he asked.

"I'm sorry for scaring you," he said and looked away.

"How many times are you gonna apologize?" she chuckled, "Yes, I was scared but now I think that was hot."

He looked at her again and she continued, "And what was that 'babe' thing and 'darling' and what more? Sweetheart, Oh my my! See, I'm still getting goosebumps." He pressed his lips together feeling a little embarrassed.

"That's so crazy man." She was being dramatic, he couldn't control his laugh.

"You are weird," he shook his head and she giggled.

"Just for you," she said, tapping her finger on his lips but suddenly he flipped her, trapping her against that wooden railing between his arms.

"Dare to do that again." He came dangerously close to her. She gulped seeing his dominating eyes. He seemed so serious still staring into her soul. Words were stuck in her throat.

"I'm s-sorry," she managed to utter.

But suddenly he started to laugh loudly, "HAHAHA!! Look at your face....HAHAHA! Cera you ar—"

Suddenly she pecked his lips still with those scared expressions, causing him to laugh more. She blinked and looked away but she smiled slightly hitting on his chest.

"HA HA! Had fun?" she asked sarcastically.

"Hey .... I was just kidding. You are so cute." He hugged her from the back.

They both stayed like that, closing their eyes. They were feeling each other's warmth.

"Jimmy?"

"Hmm...."

"I wanna know about you," she said but heard a pause and then he spoke, "I'll tell you, I need some time. Will you wait for me?"

"It's ok. I'll wait for you. You trust me, right?" She turned around and hugged him.

"Yes, I do," he said kissing the top of her head to assure her.

Chapter 17

After delivering some cakes for a birthday party, Jimmy and Cera were roaming around while holding hands.

"Cera, stop looking at me like that, it's embarrassing. Everyone is looking at us."

Cera gasped, "How mean!" and she pouted, looking away.

"Aww! Honey, look at them. They look so cute together, don't they?" An unknown lady asked her husband while looking at Jimmy and Cera.

"Yeah, muffin with mochi." She laughed at her husband's comment. Hearing them, Jimmy and Cera also laughed.

"Yes, sweet couple."

"T-thanks, Aunty," Jimmy said shyly as he didn't know what to say and Cera was not saying anything.

"Aww... look at him, he is blushing. Your husband is so cute, sweetie."

Jimmy's eyes slightly widened hearing the lady but Cera was smiling from ear to ear.

"H-Husband? Aun-"

"Yes, my husband is really shy," Cera said, clinging to Jimmy and making him completely shy.

"Bless you two," she patted Cera's head and the couple left from there.

And Cera looked at Jimmy who was already looking at her completely stunned but she smiled and blinked at him innocently, "Let's go, hubby."

He chuckled, shaking his head, "You are crazy."

"Just for you." They both laughed and went out.

As soon as they came out, Cera saw....

"TOYO!"

Her beloved car. She ran towards it, and Jimmy followed, confused.

"Toyo! I missed you, baby," she said kissing and caressing the car.

"Cera, what are you doing?"

"Jimmy, it's my car. My baby, it's- wait, what are you doing here? Is my dad here?" Cera suddenly became alert and carefully started looking around. Jimmy was not understanding as Cera was talking with a black sports car.

But a man approached them, "Hey, what are you doing?" He said pushing Cera aside but Jimmy caught her before she fell.

"Hey! What are—"

"HOW DARE YOU TO TOUCH ME?" Moving Jimmy away, Cera went to grab that man's collar.

"This is my TOYO! My car!" Cera was throwing attitude, Jimmy was trying to pull her back.

Man scoffed, "What? Before saying that, first look at yourself."

Cera gasped madly, "What do you mean YOU PUNK—"

"Cera, stop it!" Jimmy held her back as she was about to punch the man.

"Hah- do you even know to whom this car belongs? Billionaire businessman Mr. Fo—" That man stopped before taking a name, "It's his daughter's favourite car. I'm just its caretaker. One scratch on this car and I'm dead. So back off!"

Cera scoffed, "And do you know who I am?"

He rolled his eyes, "Who?"

"I'm the one who—" Cera stopped and gulped hard on her words.

"What?"

"N-Nothing," Cera said looking away.

"Yes, Nothing. You are nothing," the man chuckled and getting into the car, he drove off.

"Am I really n-nothing?" Cera asked herself while looking at the car leaving.

"No, you are the owner of 'Cera's Delights." Cera heard Jimmy from behind and felt his hand on her shoulder.

She smiled and turned around, "And what's that?"

"You are going to open a cake shop, right? So this is the name for your shop," he said with a smile.

"Nice," she said, still smiling at him realizing how caring and understanding he was.

He held her hand as they both started to walk while talking.

"I talked for hours while sitting inside it, whenever I felt down or wanted someone to talk to, I felt like it was always hearing me. It was my friend. I shared everything with it. I talked about you also," Cera chuckled sadly while talking about her car to Jimmy.

It was not a big deal or a thing to get concerned about but Jimmy was still listening to her and was understanding her emotions with her car.

"I used to go out in my Toyo, sneaking out of the house in the middle of the night," she sighed.

Suddenly, Jimmy crouched in front of her, she stopped walking, looking at him confusedly.

"Wanna try to ride?"

Cera smiled and gladly hopped on his back. He started to walk, "Am I heavy?" she asked.

"Yeah, so heavy," he teased.

"Why are you mean to me?" She playfully slapped on his shoulder and he laughed.

"Ok, you are not heavy, because I'm strong. I can carry you like this for the rest of my life."

Cera's heart fluttered hearing that from him. That was something he said for the first time. And she knew he meant it.

"Mwahh! Mwahh! Mwahh!" She started to kiss him on both of his cheeks. He giggled and she hugged him tightly, burying her face in his neck.

"Cera?"

"Yeah?"

"Do you want your car back?" he asked, unsure about something.

"Nope! I like this ride much more," she said swaying her legs.

He smiled, "Okay."

Chapter 18

Jimmy was at work singing when his boss suddenly approached him.

"Jimmy, today we have some special guests and they want you to serve them."

Jimmy looked at him confused. "But boss that's not my work," he said trying not to sound rude.

"Yeah I know but they want you to serve them," his boss said showing him who were the guests.

Jimmy gulped seeing some familiar faces. His breath hitched when they waved at him.

"I guess you know them. Then c'mon, just for today," his boss requested.

"But boss I d—"

"No buts Jimmy. I'll pay extra for it. Please do it for our service's reputation."

Jimmy didn't know what to say as his boss was pleading.

"O-Ok."

Jimmy took a serving tray and a bottle of wine and started to walk towards them.

"Hi! Long time no see, Jimmy Tolger," a man in a black suit said with a smirk. Jimmy didn't say anything and just offered him a drink.

"Bro, he got guts. Don't you think?" another boy said to him.

"I guess, Sonki," the boy in black said, side-eying Jimmy.

They took drinks. There were some girls too with them.

"Rocky, do you know this cutie?" one of the girls asked the boy in black.

"Yeah, we know him very well. He's our old friend," Rocky's sarcasm was clearly visible.

"Ohhh a friend," she said and blew smoke on Jimmy's face. Jimmy moved back coughing a little.

She tugged on Jimmy's sleeve and made him sit beside her. "We don't know each other, I'm Laura and you, cutie?" she said, trailing her finger on his face while others were just smirking enjoying Jimmy's helpless state. But Jimmy gulped and moved away.

"I'm s-sorry, Ma'am but I-I have s-some work," Jimmy said getting up, but she again pulled him back down to sit.

"C'mon, I can take you somewhere else for some more important work," she whispered to Jimmy but others heard it too and they chuckled. Jimmy shivered, he was feeling so uncomfortable as she was touching him.

"Why not? That's what his actual business is," Sonki said and they all laughed.

Jimmy's heart dropped, he was holding himself from falling into any trauma again.

"Really? Then that'll be more fun," she said leaning on Jimmy.

"No!" Jimmy got up, pushing her away but ended up accidentally spilling her drink on her expensive dress, she gasped. Jimmy's eyes widened as he didn't mean to do it.

Tears were already starting to form in Jimmy's eyes.

"How dare you!" She yelled and Jimmy flinched.

Jimmy's boss approached them, "What's wrong, Jimmy?"

"Is this your service? He poured all the drink on my dress! Do you know how expensive it is?" She started to shout at Jimmy's boss madly.

"No b-boss, I didn't mean t-to do that. I-I acc- I'm sorry, Ma'am," Jimmy said, continuously bowing.

"I'm sorry on his behalf, Ma'am. He didn't mean to do so. It was an accident," his boss also apologized.

"Sorry? Are you gonna pay for this?" She was mad.

"I can't afford ma'am, please forgive me," Jimmy was holding back his sobs as he was already on the verge.

"You can afford it if you pay me in another way, cutie," she smirked and said, coming closer to Jimmy.

Jimmy gulped and looked at his boss and then looked away, feeling embarrassed.

"I'll try to get you new service," his boss excused himself and left from there.

"C'mon boy, be a man! That's not hard for you, right?" Rocky said putting a hand on Jimmy's shoulder.

Jimmy moved away slowly shaking his head while looking down. He was not able to speak as he was losing his mind.

"It's not like it's your first time. You have done these things before also, even forcefully." Sonki was laughing.

But Jimmy's heart was breaking into pieces. They were trying to trigger Jimmy.

"You know, Laura, his mom was also in the same business. He doesn't even know who his father is," Rocky said to the girl who was flirting with Jimmy. They were laughing and humiliating Jimmy. But Jimmy couldn't hear anything bad about his mom.

"And his mom is blind so she also can't tell him who wa—"

And that's it. Losing his patience, Jimmy grabbed Sonki's collar and punched him hard.

"How dare you speak about my mom like that!" Jimmy was mad and started punching Sonki. Rocky tried to stop him. Jimmy's boss and other staff also gathered there hearing the chaos.

Rocky moved Jimmy away from Sonki and started to beat him like he was waiting for this moment, "How dare you? You dirty piece! He spits what the truth is!" Rocky was being so cruel that he forgot Jimmy was human.

Hearing Rocky and others saying those bad things, Jimmy started to lose his senses, he started to tremble in fear.

"Stop it, sir! You can't do this! I need to call the cops!" Jimmy's boss said while trying to stop them, but Rocky didn't stop. It was like he was taking out all his anger.

"No please.... I d-didn't do a-anything wrong.... I-I didn't...... It h-hurts, please stop," Jimmy was in pain. He was completely traumatized by something. He was crying hard, begging them to stop.

After some time at home

Cera came to answer the phone call, thinking it might be one of her customers but it was from Jack.

On the phone

"Hey, ssup! What ar-" Her heart shook hearing what Jack said.

"What? Which hospital?"

"Yeah, I'm coming." She hung up and removing her apron she ran out.

Chapter 19

"Ok, I think we should just talk to him—"

Jack came with Mike to the club where Jimmy worked but they saw how brutally Rocky was beating Jimmy, "Jimmy!" Jack ran to save his friend and so did Mike.

"HEY! HEY! STOP IT! I SAID STOP IT!!" Jack pulled Rocky away from Jimmy, but Rocky pushed Jack away too. Having no option left, Jack grabbed Rocky by his collar, threw him on the bar and started punching him.

Mike ran to check on Jimmy. Jimmy was badly beaten and he was crying miserably, "P-Please I d-didn't do anything.....d-don't hurt me p-please ...."

"No. No one will hurt you, Jimmy, Calm down!" Mike was feeling bad looking at Jimmy's condition, that Jimmy was not able to even recognize anyone. Mike's heart clenched.

Suddenly, security guards entered and separated Jack and Rocky. Jack ran straight to Jimmy, "Jimmy." Jack was so worried seeing all the bruises on Jimmy's face.

"Jimmy, it's me, Jack," but Jimmy was crying, not able to process anything in his mind.

"Hey... hey look at me, it's me, Jack. C'mon." Jack patted Jimmy's cheek to make him conscious. Hearing Jack's voice, Jimmy held his hand tightly.

"Jack, y-you know, right? I-I d-didn't do anything..... I didn't h-hurt anyone.....you k-know ...p-please tell t-them not to h-hurt me."

Jack's heart was breaking hearing Jimmy, he knew what was happening to Jimmy but he didn't know how to comfort him, tears filled Jack's eyes seeing his friend in a helpless state.

Jack gulped hard before speaking, "Y-yeah, I know. You have done nothing wrong. I believe you, don't panic, ok? Calm down! No one will hurt you.... you are safe Jimmy."

Jimmy hugged Jack tightly, like he was the safest place for him. Jack was caressing him to calm him down.

"What's happening to him? We need to take him to hospital. He is injured," Mike said as he was worried for Jimmy.

Jack nodded, "But first he needs to calm down, he won't move from here till then."

Mike called his driver to bring the car. Jack glared at Rocky who was being stopped by guards.

"How inhuman you are! How long are you gonna play with him? LEAVE HIM ALONE! You have hurt him enough! Don't you see the pain he is suffering?" Jack knew who Rocky was, as something like this had happened before also.

"It's nothing! You don't know what he has done to me! I'll make him suffer more! He has to suffer more!" Rocky was trying to storm towards Jack but the guards were holding him back.

"But he never intended to hurt you in any way... he was the one—" Jack was mad too but Mike stopped him.

"Not now, Jack, We need to take Jimmy to the hospital," Mike said and saw Jimmy was already unconscious.

Then they heard the police siren as Jimmy's boss had already reported about Rocky.

Jack quickly carried Jimmy to Mike's car to take him to the hospital. On the way, Jack informed Cera.

After some time at the hospital

Jimmy was not with anyone. He was just curled up on the bed with his eyes closed, avoiding the people around him. Jack tried to talk with him but he was not responding well.

"He's fine, give him some time."

Hearing the doctor, Mike nodded, "Thank you, doctor." The doctor went out.

And Jack entered. He saw Jimmy was still backing him. Jack knew Jimmy was embarrassed by himself and was getting the wrong thoughts, but Jack knew he just needed some time.

"But why was he acti—" Mike was about to ask something but Jack pulled him out.

"It's his trauma, it always makes him weak. As much as he tries to be strong, it always breaks him that hard. It's really messing up with his life," Jack explained and Mike sighed.

"I don't know about his past but I really want him to come to life again and make it better for himself and his loved ones," Mike said and Jack nodded in agreement.

"Jack?"

"Cera..." Jack saw Cera, her tired figure suggested that she had come running all the way to the hospital.

"Cera? Cera Ford?" Mike was confused seeing her there. Mike knew who Cera was as he had seen her at one of her father's parties.

Cera came towards them, her red eyes clearly showing that she'd cried all the way here, "W-Where is he? What happened to h-him?"

"He is fine now. You can meet him, He is inside and..." Jack wiped her tears and cleaned her face "Don't cry in front of him, he needs your strength and I know how strong you are! And don't ask him anything, ok?"

Cera nodded and went inside to see Jimmy. Jack turned to Mike who seemed confused.

"Cera Ford, right? But she was missing from fe—" Mike said but Jack sighed.

"Come, sit....." Jack and Mike sat there on the bench and Jack told him everything about Cera's story as Mike had become a good friend of his and he could trust him.

Chapter 20

Cera came inside and saw he was sleeping. She sat near him on the bed.

"Jimmy...."

She called him, he lifted his wet eyelids. Tilting her head a little, she gave him a small smile. But he looked away and tried to get up so she helped him. She saw his bruised face, and her heart clenched. He was not looking at her and was trying to hide those IVs in his hand. She noticed but didn't say anything.

Cera cupped his face trying hard not to break emotions, "Ayyi! My baby," she caressed him with a sad pout.

"Is it hurting a lot? It's ok, you'll be fine," she kissed his cheek, but he was still not saying anything.

Cera was mad at those people who had hurt Jimmy but she didn't want to bring that topic in front of him, so for now she was just distracting him, but seeing him like that was breaking her heart too and she hugged him.

As soon as she hugged him, her tears fell but she wiped them quickly when she felt him hugging her back. She was trying hard to play it cool and Jimmy was also controlling himself from breaking in front of her, he was holding his tears back and she didn't fail to notice that. His hug was tightening around her, burying his face deeper into her neck. And she finally heard his sniffles.

Gulping on the lump in her throat, she caressed his back.

"I know, y-you are not l-liking it here. We'll g-go home soon, ok? D-Don't cry..." She bit hard on her lip to prevent herself from letting out a sob. Jimmy was trying to be silent but Cera could feel his sobs hitting on her neck.

But her presence was helping him calm down, he was feeling that comfort in her.

The next day at home

"How mean! I went there for you..."

"And got Mr. Song's stick on your ass." Cera and Jack started to laugh talking about some of their funny memories.

They were trying to lose that tensed aura of Jimmy who was not talking at all. Cera looked at Jimmy, he was not even eating but just staring at the food. She looked at Jack concerned, Jack just gave her a slow blink.

"Jimmy, isn't the food good? I made it for you. Sorry, I tried it for the first time and Jack also helped me."

"Yeah, but it's really good. I was also thinking it would be horrible but it's nice. Try it." Jack looked at Cera as Jimmy still didn't say anything.

Jimmy was not listening to them but.....

"That's what his business is....."

"His mom was in the same business....."

"He doesn't even know who his father is....."

Tears again fell from his eyes, his hands were shaking. But suddenly he flinched when he felt someone's hand on his.

"Jimmy....?"

Jimmy looked up at Jack.

"You should eat something," Jack said but Jimmy got up and left from there.

"Jimmy?" Cera was about to follow him but Jack stopped her.

"Relax. He'll be fine, he is trying his best. He still needs some time."

Cera just looked at Jimmy's room, worried. She felt a pat on her back by Jack.

"Ok, I'll leave now. Try to talk to him. I didn't say anything to Mom. She is with Mike's Mom. I dropped her at Mike's home so you two can have some time. So use it," Jack said getting up and patting her head. He sighed, "I know I can also tell you about him but I want him to tell you because now, you are someone to him who he wants to trust the most, who he should trust the most."

Cera was so touched by Jack's words and how mature and understanding he was.

"Thank you, Jack." It's all she could say for now.

He smiled and went out, leaving her again in her deep thoughts.

But then suddenly she heard some kind of a loud thud. Her eyes widened.

"Jimmy!"

She ran to the bedroom to see Jimmy.

But when she came to his room, Jimmy wasn't there. Then she heard the sound of running water from the bathroom.

Pushing the door open of the bathroom, when Cera entered inside she saw a shelf had fallen, spreading shampoo bottles and soaps all over the tiles. Then she saw Jimmy, who was shivering under the cold shower, curling himself on the floor. He was choking on his sobs.

She ran to him and embraced him, "Jimmy, please calm down.... Don't think of anything."

"Cera ....I-I never hurt a-anyone, I swear.... I-I'm not bad. T-They were saying b-bad things a-about mom. W-Why are they h-hurting me this w-way?" He was messed up. "It hurts Cera.... Hurts so much..."

Cera's heart was breaking more hearing him but she was trying to collect herself for him.

"Shuu! No one will hurt you ever again.... Don't think about those things. You are not weak.... Calm your mind, Jimmy. Think about me— Think about us. I-I'm always here...I believe in you. You can never do anything bad."

Jimmy hugged her waist tightly. But he was not calming down, and he was getting kind of fits. Cera didn't know what to do or how to comfort him. Seeing his condition, she was also getting panicked but suddenly moving him back she attached her lips to his while slowly caressing his scalp. She found him kissing her back and his muscles started to relax.

Cera heard him murmuring something, "Shuu!" She continued caressing his back. "It's only you and me, think about us only," she managed to say between kisses. He pulled her closer. His sobs faded as he started to calm down.

After sometime

Cera saw Jimmy had changed and she smiled at him, but he looked away. He was even avoiding eye contact with her as he was so embarrassed. She got him a towel and went to him to dry his hair.

"I'll d-do it," he said taking the towel from her but still, she took it back from him and made him sit on the bed.

"Let me do it," and she started to dry his hair.

So he just sat there feeling a little relaxed.

"Are you feeling better?" she asked.

"Y-Yeah...."

"Let's go on a date today, what say?" she asked a little excitedly, but he looked at her smiling face, blinked and then looked away.

"Yes... So I'll get read—"

"Cera...."

She looked at him.

"I'm not sure, I-I don't want to g-go out," he said. She knew he'd say something like this.

But she was also 'The Cera.'

"Please, Jimmy, I really want to go somewhere. I also don't have any work or orders today so I have time too. I don't know when I will get such time again," she requested but he still didn't seem sure. "You'll also feel better... please," and this was the real reason she wanted to go out.

Jimmy stared at her as she made cute faces with puppy eyes.

Chapter 21

On Cera's insistence, Jimmy came with her on their first date at Cera's favourite place.

"And from here we ca- OMG! COTTON CANDY! THAT'S SO CUTE! JIMMY I WANT IT!" Cera shouted out after suddenly talking normally, startling Jimmy and gaining some attention from around.

Cera noticed Jimmy's shocked face and looked around laughing awkwardly and he chuckled shaking his head after what felt like.... years.

"Haha.... but I've never tried it, I just saw it from afar. And these look cute, see?" she said looking at the kids who were playing with different shapes of cotton candies.

"I want it." She pouted cutely, fluttering his heart in the same way after long. He looked at her for a moment and smiled.

"Why are you like this? Let's go," he held her hand and went to get candy for her. She looked at him and smiled.

At least he was trying for her.

Cera got a huge bear-shaped candy. She was looking at it fascinatedly like a kid, "This is so cute, do I really need to bite on it?"

"Ok fine... Excuse me, we don't wa-" Jimmy said taking it from her and was about to return but she stopped him.

"Hey! No! I want it!" She pouted. Jimmy shook his head at her silliness and got one for himself too.

He took a bite of his cotton candy but she was looking at him and he gave her a side eye, "What?"

"Jimmy, Can I have a bite from yours? I really don't wanna ruin mine."

He looked at her weirdly, "N-NO! Eat yours, I won't give you mine," he said turning away from her. She pressed her lips, enjoying the way he was acting cute. So she teased him more.

"It will be ruined, see how cute it is!" she said showing her bear to him.

"It's gonna ruin anyways, even if you don't eat it, Cera."

"Don't be so mean Jimmy," she said holding his hand in an attempt to eat his candy but he was moving his hand away. He stretched his hand up as she tried to catch it while jumping, he was also in full mood to tease her.

And suddenly he ran.

"Hey! Jimmy Tolger!" She started to chase him.

His laugh was clearly heard as he was running away from her and she followed him smiling.

"Cera, why are you so STUBBORN?"

"Jimmy, STOP right there! NOW I ONLY WANT THAT CANDY IN YOUR HAND," hearing her, he laughed more, but suddenly Cera tripped and fell on the grass, and her candy also fell along with her.

Jimmy stopped and looked behind to see her. She was on the grass so it didn't hurt her much.

"Ayyi! You ok?" he asked, crouching near her. She folded her arms and pouted and he chuckled, "Now what are you gonna eat?" He showed his candy to her. which was also all liquid sugar.

"Hehe, let's get one more for you," he said, helping her get up.

"No."

"Huh- but you wanted to ha-" He stopped speaking when she pulled him close by his hoodie and touched her lips to his, slightly biting on them.

He was frozen until she moved back and smiled at him. He blinked slowly for a few seconds and his eyes slightly widened realizing she could see his pink cheeks.

"That was sweet," she said winking at him. He blushed and looked away.

"There are people a-around, what a-are you doing?" he said scratching his forehead. She laughed at the way he was flustered.

"Aww.... so what? You are my boyfie! Mah Cutie!" she said squishing his cheeks between her palms making a plump pout of his lips and was about to peck on it but before that, he dragged her away from there.

But they were all unaware that someone's eyes were on them.

On the phone

"Yeah, she is here in front of my eyes. But there is someone with her." A man in all black with black goggles said into his microphone.

"Who?"

He heard from the other side.

"A boy," he replied.

"Jack Pros?"

"No. He is not Jack. Someone else. Looks like her boyfriend," he replied after a pause.

"Keep your eyes on them."

"Ok," said the man in black, hanging up.

Chapter 22

Holding hands....
 Stepping along....
Moist cold breezes were hitting her face, slightly messing her hair. She tugged the blowing strands of hair behind her ear while walking on the seashore looking at the pleasing sunset. The ticklish sensation of the water touching her feet and Jimmy's eyes on her, made everything feel like a dream.

Was it really a dream?

Cera stopped, and so did he. He had that smile on his face all the time while admiring her but he also noticed some kind of worry in her eyes.

"What happened?" he asked.

She forced a smile and looked around. "Let's sit there," she said pointing at a place. They walked towards there and settled themselves.

Cera was looking straight at the setting sun and Jimmy was looking at her glowing face with the sunlight. He also noticed that as the sun was setting, her expressions were setting too. He tilted his head to get her attention. She saw him and gulped when he raised his eyebrows, silently asking her what was wrong.

"Why are you so silent suddenly?" he asked.

"I'm happy," she replied.

He frowned with a confused smile.

"It scares me whenever I feel so happy, it feels like a dream."

Jimmy was still confused not knowing what she was talking about.

"But you are not dreaming, Cera."

She slowly hugged his arm resting her head on his shoulder.

"But it's for sure that I can't be happy for long." She sounded worried, and Jimmy felt her hug tightening around his arm. He wrapped his arm around her shoulder, pulling her closer. He didn't know why she was talking like that all of a sudden.

"No. You have to be happy with your whole heart for me and I'll try my best not to make you sad again. I promise," he said holding her hand and kissing it.

And finally, he managed to bring that beautiful smile to her face.

Time skipped

"And he divorced my mom when I was just a kid. My mom didn't have enough money to raise me so he got my custody. In the beginning, he was good to me but after a few years he started to ignore me completely." Cera was talking about her mom and dad. Jimmy was listening to her attentively, comforting her.

"And after two years, my mom got into an accident and died...... but you know, I don't think it was an accident. She killed herself. She was not able to live alone." Cera was trying hard not to cry. And she chuckled sadly.

"But I learnt to live without both of them. Finding myself and living only for myself. And then I met you, the actual reason for me to live." She smiled in tears looking at him.

Jimmy felt that lump in his throat. He looked into her eyes which were full of hope and with lots of love and care. And that was scaring Jimmy for some reason. He looked at their intertwined hands.

"Cera."

"Hmm."

"Don't think of me as your reason to live, be yourself. Live for yourself again," he said lowering his head.

She kissed his hand, "Nope! Now that I have you in my life, why should I live my life alone again? Jimmy, you are my reason to be happy and why should I quit on that?"

"And why are you talking like you are going to vanish?" she said making him look at her. "Don't you still trust me, Jimmy? Will you leave me?"

He stared at her glittering eyes, pleading with him. "No. I trust you Cera and I'll never leave you," he said pulling her closer to his chest.

"I won't leave you, Cera, I don't want to leave you ever but.....
I'm scared, what if you want to leave me?"

Jimmy sighed thinking to himself but suddenly they heard a bell. They looked up and saw an ice cream truck. Cera looked at Jimmy and he got it and smiled, "Stay here, I'll bring one for you."

Jimmy went to get ice cream for Cera and Cera sat there on the bench waiting for him. And then some boys came to Cera while she was alone, her alert button got pressed because they seemed to be not so good. She stood up and looked at Jimmy, but he was a little far away on the other side of the ice cream truck, from where he was not able to see Cera.

"Hi," a boy in a brown leather jacket smiled at her and asked, "Are you Jimmy's girlfriend?"

Cera smiled a little, thinking of them as Jimmy's friends as they were smiling, "Umm, yeah. Are you guys his friends?"

"Well, yeah. I'm Rocky."

"Oh, hi," Cera said still looking for Jimmy. "Jimmy went to get ice-"

"Are you really his girlfriend? Or you are rich and he's again just using you?", Sonki said, there 5-6 guys were laughing together. Cera couldn't understand what's so funny, they were giving her the exact vibe which she was thinking a while ago.

"Hey, don't say like that Sonki", Rocky said.

"What?", Cera looked at them in disbelief on the way they were talking.

"Is he paying you?", Sonki said and Rocky also laughed.

"No bro, I think she's the one who is paying him"

They were laughing on Cera , Cera was getting angry feeling their disgusting vibes.

"What The Fuck are you talking about?", Cera stormed on them madly.

"Hahaha.... I think she doesn't know anything yet. WAKE UP GIRL! WAKE UP!HE IS JUST USING YOU! YOU DON-" Sonki was saying while shaking Cera grabbing on her shoulder. She pushed him away. They were laughing making fun of her like she was some kind of joke to them.

"Get Lost! LEAVE ME ALONE!", Cera yelled and again looked for Jimmy but he was still not there.

"We are just worried for you babe, we want to make you aware of the monster you are living with. He is not good. I'm way to better than him", Rocky said coming near Cera and held her wrist. Cera tried to jerk his hand away but his grip was strong.

"What are you doing? leave me!", Cera was struggling.

"Seems like you are also sluty like him, huh? But don't worry you don't need to pay me, If you want I can pay you as much as you want for one night, what say?", Rocky was touching her face.

Cera was confused, scared and disgusted with his touch. Tears filled in her eyes and she heard a weak voice from behind.....

"C-Cera...."

Chapter 23

"C-Cera"

Cera turned and saw Jimmy, Rocky smirked without letting go of Cera's wrist. Jimmy had heard all the things they were saying to Cera, he saw the way Rocky was holding Cera's wrist. His eyes met with Rocky's which were nothing but hate and anger.

But then Rocky let go of Cera's hand. Jimmy gulped when Cera ran towards him, "Jimmy, They are not your friends, right? They were talking very cheap things about us".

Jimmy was not able to utter a single as he was controlling himself so much, he was not over from yesterday's incident and they were here again to hurt him more. He looked at her, tears were stuck in his eyes, "L-Let's go from h-here".

Cera was confused with Jimmy, all day he was good and suddenly he changed, he was turning red like he was controlling on his tears so hard. He held her hand, she noticed even his hand was shaking.

"Why so hurry my friend? Don't you wanna have a moment with us? At least introduce us to you girlfriend properly", Rocky said and Cera stopped hearing his sarcastic words.

"No! I don't want any introduction with people like you. You know what, we don't have time for your bullshits", Cera turned around madly. And they again laughed annoying her more.

"C-Cera, Let's go....", Jimmy literally murmured as even his voice wasn't coming out.

"Yeah Yeah, how long are you gonna run away from the sins you have done?", Jimmy's heart clenched hearing Rocky and Cera was not in mood to leave from there until teaching them good lesson.

"What sins, huh? I think you are talking about yourself. You are the real sinner, it's on your face and I can smell it from you!", Cera was mad with their behavior and the way they were talking with Jimmy. But she felt Jimmy's grip tightening on her hand.

"Cera, p-please , I want to go-"

"Why don't you tell your girlfriend about your Ex-girlfriends?", Rocky again said knowing that Jimmy wanted to go from there.

Till now Cera was sure that Jimmy knew those guys and they were not good to him at all. But she was confused with the things they were talking.

"Or Are you planning to do same things with her also which you have done to Lexi and Mia?", Rocky said triggering on Jimmy's nerves more.

And here Jimmy lost it, he couldn't hold himself anymore tears fell from his eyes, "I-I have done n-nothing to t-them? t-b-believe me...."

"You are Monster! Devil behind that innocent face of yours!", Rocky's words were stabbing Jimmy harshly.

"N-No...I-I'm not- I didn-", Jimmy fell on his knees but Cera held him. She saw, he was trembling.

"Jimmy", She was checking on him worriedly not knowing what's happening to him, she again turned to Rocky madly.

"What are you doing? Stop it! Leave us alone!", She yelled.

Jimmy was curling himself covering his ears and closing his eyes.

"No! I won't stop! I won't let him live peacefully!", Rocky yelled back coming towards Jimmy but Cera pushed him away, "STAY AWAY!"

Rocky was also angry and his eyes were also red with tears, "He doesn't have any right to live after what h-"

"STOP IT! PLEASE STOP IT! HE IS NOT WELL, LEAVE HIM ALONE PLEASE!", Cera cried out loudly not knowing how to stop them as Jimmy's condition was going bad.

"DO YOU EVEN KNOW WHO HE IS, WHAT HE HAS DONE?", Rocky shouted. "He is rapist! He is a Psycho! He used his own friends and killed them!", Rocky broke into cry.

Jimmy became numb again hearing him. Cera's expressions fell, she looked at Jimmy and again at Rocky who was crying his heart out.

Cera was still processing, but suddenly Jimmy stood up and started to run away, her eyes widened, "Jimmy".

She collected herself and ran behind him, "Jimmy wait- Stop!"

Jimmy ran onto middle of the road losing his mind. Vehicles were highly crowded.

"JIMMY! PLEASE STOP", Cera's heart was racing seeing Jimmy running like that, she was scared that he might get hit by any vehicle.

Tears were falling from Jimmy's eyes continuously; his eyesight was completely blur. He was not thinking anything, only those sharp words were still ripping his heart. He didn't know where was he going, he just wanted to run away from there, somewhere unknown where no one can find him.

But here Cera's heart stopped when she saw a car racing towards Jimmy and she was far from him, "Jimmy!", she ran towards him but it was too late and she heard a loud honk of car, she squeezed her eyes close breathing heavily for a second everything went silent for her.

She opened eyes slowly. Car had stopped on time giving slight hit to Jimmy who was on the road but fortunately was not hurt much. Her tears fell, she sighed in relief and ran to Jimmy. People were crowding around. Cera was still terrified thinking about consequences of the huge accident which was about to happen.

She started to check on Jimmy but now she was mad on him, grabbing his caller she shook him to consciousness, "WHAT ARE YOU DOING? CONTRL YOURSELFJIMMY!"

But Jimmy looked at her like she was stranger to him. Cera saw that place was crowding and traffic was increasing there, seeing that all Jimmy was more scared, he was covering himself with his arms. Cera held his hand and helped him to get up. She dragged him away from there.

Chapter 24

"Control yourself please", Cera said worriedly cupping his face. But he just stared at her and slowly moving her hands away he started to walk, she frowned.

"Jimmy? Where are you going?"

But still he didn't answer. She stood in front of him, his confused eyes were scaring her more like he was not able to recognize her.

"WHAT HAPPENED? WHERE ARE YOU GOING?", he flinched stepping back from her by her sudden raised voice.

He started to cry like kid, "D-don't hurt me, I-I'm not bad". He was trembling in fear again. Cera didn't know how to talk with him.

"Jimmy, Calm do-"

"W-Who are you? Please g-go away...", Cera's heart shook hearing him. Jimmy was in very bad condition he was really not recognizing Cera. She needed to pull him back to senses.

"I-I want t-to go home , I w-want to go to m-my Mom....", Jimmy was looking around like a lost kid who wanted his mom.

"Jimmy.... Listen.... Listen to me, calm down. We'll talk, ok? Take deep breaths", Cera was feeling so helpless, she didn't know how to handle this situation.

"Y-You'll hurt me, go away f-from me.... Go Away!", he was trying to move her away.

"JIMMY! IT'S ME CERA! Why are you acting like this? Please stop it! I'm scared!", She shook him and hugged him tightly while crying hard.

Suddenly Jimmy blinked his eyes and felt her tight hug which was helping him to calm down.

"Cera...."

As soon as Cera heard her name she moved back to look on him. "Yeah it's me, it's me Cera".

"Cera, I-I want to go f-from here", He again hugged her and cried.

Cera was also crying but feeling relieved that at least he was recognizing her. She caressed him, she moved him back little resting her forehead on his.

"Please don't act like that. Control your fear. You are not alone Jimmy, I'm with you. I believe you no matter what they say!", She said cupping his face and kissed his head. "Try to hold yourself".

He was not saying anything but crying silently closing his eyes.

"Look at me", She wiped his tears but he didn't open his eyes.

"Jimmy, Look at me".

He slowly opened his eyes and looked into her eyes just to feel that strength, hope and lots of love and comfort.

"No need to run away, you have done nothing wrong. I trust you with my whole heart", Her each word and it's intense was showing their effect as he was calming down. She rubbed on his chest gently.

At Home :

Cera was laying on bed with Jimmy hugging her waist tightly and was crying on her chest silently. She was caressing him while repeating the same thing, "Shuu! Nothing will happen... you are safe".

"Will you leave me Cera? Y-You should. I'm not good, I-I'm just so pathetic"

It was breaking Cera's heart, "No, you are not".

"They w-will hurt you m-more if you stand with me. I told you, I'm not good person they say. I'm really not, they were insulting you, talking bad things about you and me, and I just stood there, I'm s-sorry. I Cou-", he was literally choking on his sobs. "I couldn't e-even protect you, y-you deserve better Cera. I'm s-sorry".

"No, what are you talking, huh? Have you forgotten already? You were the one who saved me, I'm here because of you. I can't imagine what would have happed to me that day if you were not there, you gave me new life that day. You are more deserving to be happy Jimmy", She wiped her tears.

"And I only love you, so don't talk like this. I'm not gonna leave you ever", she was continuously kissing his head.

His silent sobs were still hitting on her chest. She started to lose in thoughts full of curiosity, confusion and with lots of questions in her mind but she just kept stroking his hairs.

After sometime when she snapped back from her thoughts, she felt that silence. She noticed he was silent and motionless, "Jimmy, you should eat something". She was not able to see his face as it was buried in her neck. She didn't get any response so she looked down and he was sleeping.

She sighed, "it's ok, you need sleep too". Without thinking anything more she also closed her eyes giving him and herself sometime.

Chapter 25
Next Morning :

Jimmy felt little body ach and heavy head. He slowly opened his eyes lifting his head little and saw Cera, her squishy pink cheeks with small pout made him smile little. She was sleeping and those low snores were indicating how tired she was but she was holding him close, her one arm was under his head and other was wrapped around him. He was staring at her remembering about last night.

"Nothing will happen....."
"No need to run away....."
"I trust you with my whole heart....."
"I only Love You....."
"I'm not gonna leave you ever....."

"Cera, Are you my guardian angel?", He asked in a low voice, he moved little up removing her arm and he wrapped his arms around her securely and unconsciously in sleep she also pulled him close hugging him back. He pecked her head and stayed like that while thinking something.

After sometime:

Cera woke up feeling empty. She roamed her hand on the other side of the bed but that was empty. She opened her eyes and looked around but she couldn't find Jimmy anywhere. She gulped preventing herself from getting any negative or bad thoughts. She immediately got off the bed and was about to go out but then he entered with breakfast for her.

Seeing Cera little panic he gulped, "G-Good morning.....?"

She shrugged all her thoughts and smiled, "Yeah Good Morning".

He put breakfast on table and saw she was again lost in some kind of thoughts. He sat on the bed and pulled her on his lap snapping her back from her thoughts. She looked at him, He was smiling.

"Aren't you hungry?", He asked.

She nodded still staring at him, he took bowl and was about to feed her, "Are you feeling better?", She asked and hugged him.

Jimmy could see how affected Cera was because of him, he was feeling bad. "Yeah, I'm fine", he said stroking her back.

"I'm sorry, I'm troubling you so much, aren't I?", He said but she moved back from hug.

"No, You are not. I'm asking because, I just want to know if you are fine, ok?"

"Ok, Let's eat", He said started to feed her.

Again Next Day :

On Phone call :

"She is feeling good there after so long, Mike's mom and her friends are with her so don't worry", Jack said as Jimmy was worried about his Mom, she had not returned home yet.

"It's ok if she is comfortable there", Jimmy replied on his assurance.

"What about you? How are you", Jack asked, in meantime he couldn't get to talk with Jimmy as he knew Cera was with Jimmy so he was giving them time not wanting to interrupt.

"I'm feeling better now", Jimmy replied.

"And how are you two doing?", He meant about their new relationship.

"Cera is wit-"

"Who are you talking to baby? Mwahh!", Cera interrupted when Jimmy was on phone call and kissed his cheek turning it pink immediately. Jimmy looked at her with slightly wide eyes but then heard "Ahem" from the other side of phone.

"Seems like you two have got way too along", Jack teased.

"Umm, Y-Yeah", Jimmy started to blush scratching his forehead confusing Cera.

"Well, I'm happy for both of you. Have your time. See you soon", And Jack hung up.

Jimmy turned to Cera.

"Who was it?", And she asked.

"It was Jack"

"Oh, what did he say?"

"He said mom will be staying there for few more days", Jimmy said and saw Cera's eyes shined.

"It means we'll have more time together", She said wrapping her arms around his neck, he smiled.

"Jimmy, shall we tell mom about us? Or should we wait?", Cera said and saw Jimmy's smile slowly fading. But still he managed to fake one for her but she definitely caught it.

"L-Let's wait till she returns", He said so she also smiled.

"Ok".

"Do you want me to help you with today's orders?"

"There are not much but I like kitchen romance, you know", She winked at him pulling him towards kitchen. He chuckled shaking his head looking at her.

Time Skipped:

Cera and Jimmy were laying on the bed hugging each other while Jimmy was singing in his honey voice.

She asked "Are these diamonds in the sky?"

I said "yes I putt hose there for you",
She asked "Can I have the one?"
I said "It's me one out of those",
"She said "You are the brightest",
I said "It's b'coz Ishine with your light".

But Jimmy stopped singing when he saw Cera had fallen asleep. He sighed and smiled looking at her, he knew she was trying hard to comfort him and putting all those efforts to make him trust her completely not knowing he was being scared of something. Something which might destroy him completely again and this time there was no chance that he would be able to stand again.

"You look so calm when you sleep or otherwise", He chuckled and covered her pulling her closer.

"You are my angel Cera, please protect me. I'm really scared. World is scary, you know", he was talking quietly to himself while drifting to sleep.

Chapter 26

After 2 days :

"What are you doing?", Cera chuckled as she was only able to see darkness because Jimmy was covering her eyes while taking her somewhere.

"I might trip Jimmy, where are you taking me?", She again asked.

"Just in our balcony, you don't see anything, right?", Jimmy said carefully guiding her towards balcony. She laughed.

"No Jimmy, I can't see anything. But what's new in balcony? Why are you covering my eyes?", She was asking being impatient.

"You know what, you talk too much", He said.

"I know, right?", they both laugh.

"Ok, we are here, now slowly open your eyes", he said removing his hand from her eyes. And as he said she slowly started to open her eyes.

Cera's eyes shined with wide smile on her face when she saw a small cozy bed in a balcony decorated with lights, flowers and soft cushions.

"Is it our second date?", She asked narrowing her eyes.

"Umm, yeah", he said scratching back of his neck and she laughed.

Cera was admiring the way he had arranged everything so beautifully. She smiled seeing those coffee mugs.

"Do you like it?", Jimmy asked.

"I loved it", She said throwing herself on cushions. He smiled and placed himself beside her. Cera curled herself near his chest feeling his warmth as he wrapped him arms around her.

"Why so romantic today mister?", She looked up at him.

"I was always romantic, you never knew", He replied.

"Well, you never showed", she pouted and he pecked it.

"So I did today, Just for you", He said tapping his finger on her lip.

Cera suddenly flipped their positions and hovered him, "Dare To Do That Again!".

.

.

Silence

.

.

And they both busted into laugh. Cera fell on him laughing hard on her over-acting.

"You are really weird Cera".

"Just For You Jimmy".

Cera loved the way Jimmy had become so talkative to her. They were looking at each other while catching their breath as their laugh started to fade.

"Thank you, for making me laugh", Jimmy smiled stroking her hairs.

Cera smiled and leaned her head on his chest. He kissed top of her head and finally decided to say it, "Cera, I want to tell you about me. Will you listen?".

Cera closed her eyes in relief that finally he was going to do that.

"I'm always her to listen to you Jimmy, just say it", She said intertwining her hand with his.

He gulped before starting, "Seven years ago....".

"Seven years?", that's it, here her heart started to clench just by thinking that he had been suffering from seven years.

Flashback 7 years ago :

Jimmy was rehearsing for an event in which he was going to represent his school. He was playing his guitar while singing in the campus. Everyone was looking at him while losing themselves in his angelic voice. That 17 years old boy was school's heart throb. Girls were always found fan girling over him but Jimmy, He was all shy, silent and kind of introvert kid. He was always very polite and gentle with everyone, who was needed to be protected, his innocence needed to be protected.

Jimmy stopped singing and opened his eyes as everyone started to clap, he looked down being shy.

"Well done Jimmy, You are a rock star", and this was how girls were fan girling over him.

"T-Thanks", He was turning red as he didn't know that these many people were listening to him.

"Just tell me you are single already", Someone said from the crowd.

"No, I don't think there's any chance for you Becky, He is already dating his guitar", and they laughed so did Jimmy.

"Hey! Jimmy! Is there some kind of concert going on that you are flexing your skills here?"

Jimmy rolled his eyes when he heard his annoying friend coming there moving people aside from her way.

"Stop over reacting Lexi, I was just practicing", Jimmy said putting his guitar inside the bag.

"Yeah Yeah, but why here? You can practice in hall too, just to sh-",She stop speaking as he was silent. "What's wrong?", She asked.

"Don't talk like this, I'm already nervous", Jimmy sighed.

"Shut up ok, those claps were for you. I talk like this because you are super talented. So you better calm down and no need to be nervous mah Chubby!",Lexi said pulling his cheeks.

"Will you be there in final rehearsal? I'll feel less burden", He asked, she paused looking at him but she smiled and nodded.

"Hey Lexi!"

Lexi's eyes widened hearing the voice and she immediately squeezed them, Jimmy chuckled on her reaction.

"Here comes Mr. Romeo, I mean Mr. Rocky", Jimmy whispered to Lexi, Lexi slapped on his shoulder before turning to Rocky.

"Hi Lexi, Hi Jimmy", Rocky said approaching them.

"Hey Rocky", Jimmy smiled and Lexi also gave the forced one.

"Beautiful flowers for a beautiful girl", Rocky said giving flowers to Lexi.

"Umm, Thanks Rocky", Lexi said again with that fake smile. Jimmy though the was third wheeling so decided to leave.

"I'll see you later, I have class", Jimmy excused and was about leave but Lexi grabbed on his bag and stopped him.

"Umm yeah, I also have some work, I'll also leave. So, See you around bye", Lexi said but tried not to sound rude.

"But Lexi, I was- Ok bye", Rocky couldn't complete as Lexi pulled Jimmy away from there. Rocky pouted looking down.

Chapter 27

"Hey, why do you keep him hanging like that? Why don't you just answer him? He seems to be changed, He confessed to you and also giving you time to think. What's wrong with you?", Jimmy asked Lexi while they were walking towards home after school.

"Yeah, I know Jimmy but..... but I don't feel anything for him. He is not good boy, Not my type".

Jimmy laughed, "Then at least tell him that 'He Is Not Your Type', so he won't bother you anymore".

"Hmm, I'll but let's see how long he try", She replied.

"No, this is bad thing Lexi. You should not play with someone like this".

She paused smiling at him, "Ok".

Jimmy knew, Lexi always hated this relationship things and her saying' Rocky was not her type' was just excuse to avoid it. So Jimmy decided to tease her more.

"What is your TYPE by the way?", He asked to piss her but....

"You".

Jimmy stopped hearing her so did she.

"I Love You", she again said. Jimmy gulped and looked away.

And seeing his reaction she corrected herself, "As a best friend". He smiled. She knew Jimmy was still young and younger than her too. His shy nature will make him awkward around her.

"Umm, I'll take more time to think", She changed the topic.

"Are you really gonna think about Rocky?", He asked little surprised and she nodded.

"Ok, take your time", He said patting her shoulder.

Time skipped at home:

"Eat well baby, you are busy in rehearsals in school plus study stuffs are different too. I know you don't even get time to eat anything", Ella said feeding her son more.

"No Mom, I eat in school. I don't skip any meal so please I'm full now", He said stopping his mom from stuffing his mouth and he got up.

"This kid", She shook her head.

"Mom, will you come to the event?", he asked, she smiled.

"Of course I'll", She said finding his head and he quickly knelt in front of her. She caressed him.

"I'm so proud of you my son".

"Huh? But I have not done anything yet mom, Event is next month", He said and she chuckled.

"Ayy, I'm proud you because you are the most beautiful and innocent soul in this world, not like other people", She said caressing his hairs so he rested his head on her lap.

"It's because you have taught me good things mom, You taught me to be a good person. You taught me not to take advantage of anyone's bad condition and also not to hurt anyone's feelings. You taught me how to be a human and how to treat other well and many more, so I'm proud of you mom", hearing him Ella laughed as he always repeated these things like a lesson. He smiled.

"But you are too innocent for this world Jimmy, Sometime you should not be all naive and try to see the real world", Ella said little worried but Jimmy didn't understand but, "Ok Mom".

Time skipped to Mid-Night :

Hearing some crash in the middle of the night Ella went to check on Jimmy.

"Jimmy? What happened?", She asked coming inside the room.

"N-Nothing mom, I-I a-accidently hit lamp and it b-broke, I'm sorry mom?", He replied trying to keep his voice as stable as he could.

"It's ok, are you hurt?", She asked but didn't get any reply.

"Jimmy? Are-"

"Yes M-mom, I-I'm fine", He said but she understood.

Finding her way she approached her son and slowly pulled him in a hug. She caressed him when she heard sniffles.

"Are you ok? Did you again get nightmare?", She asked knowing he was scared and trying his best to control his fear not wanting to make his mom worried but she was mother, she would know anyhow.

Jimmy nodded hugging his mom back.

"It's ok, it was just a nightmare Jimmy, no need to be scared. Don't cry", She said trying to comfort him.

Jimmy always got this kind of nightmares, he was not like other normal kids. He was way too sensitive than other boys, he was not much mentally strong. He was shy but little scared to approach new people, because of that he didn't have much friends. Ella didn't know what childhood trauma he was suffering through. But it was not any trauma but Jimmy had been listening to those bad things people used to say about him and his mom made him scared of people and made that scenario in his mind about society. He felt bad for his mom when he was growing understanding many things about his existence.

Ella had been always protecting Jimmy even though she was not completely able to do so. She always tried to keep Jimmy away from all negativity. She didn't want any bad shadow steal her son's innocent soul.

As a single mother Ella's life wasn't easy. It was hard for her to answer Jimmy whenever he asked her about his father because she herself didn't knew who was his father. Ella was born blind. Her family was poor and was not so supportive. Her stepfather had sold her in strippers club but somehow with the help of someone she managed to escape from there not knowing the person who was helping was nothing but filthy monster just like those people who she was running from. And that day something happened which was enough to destroy her life, like a huge thunder slammed on her. Without shelter, without any family or any support she was just like waiting for her death. But suddenly a small ray of hope shine in her dark life which was Jimmy. Ella was given a shelter by some charity trust and she started to work for them and there she found out that she was pregnant with Jimmy. People talked bad things about her, about her child but still she decided to keep the child and raise him the way she wanted.

Even though Ella had found some good people in her life who at least helped her to live but She had seen the worst side of the world and she didn't want her child to face those things. She didn't want her son to be surrounded with those evil heartless people or to be like one of them. Somewhere she was scared as Jimmy was boy, she didn't want Jimmy do be a man like his father. Because that was traumatic even though she was happy with Jimmy right now.

Ella had been still working for the same charity office as receptionist and sometimes Jimmy also worked there to help her. She earns enough for herself and Jimmy but never get to provide some extra things to her son like other parents do to appreciate their child, she always felt bad about that but Jimmy also never asked anything more knowing and understanding with the situation. He had started to work part time but his mom didn't allow him to do so and told him to focus on studies.

Jimmy wanted to give his mom good life because now at this age it was hard for him to see his mom working so hard for him, even though he was still too young to get some good paying jobs, so he made his talent a way, to achieve what he had dreamt of.

Singing and dancing was Jimmy's passion like he couldn't breath without music. He was quite popular in his school.

And this was how his life going. He was happy while chasing his dreams, happy while living in that moment to make unforgettable memories not knowing soon these memories were going to be his worst nightmares.

Chapter 28

Few days later:

"Hey, May I sit here?", a girl asked approaching Jimmy seeing him sitting alone.

He looked up and gave her small smile, "Yeah s-sure".

"I'm Mia, your new classmate, if you know", she smiled taking seat in front of him.

"Yeah I'm Jimmy, Hello".

"Why are you sitting alone?", she asked.

"No, actluly my friend will be here soon. Her class is going long I guess, she'll be he-" he got interrupted.

"Hey Tolger!", Jimmy and Mia turned to the voice and saw Lexi at the entrance of cafeteria.

Throwing her bag on her shoulder Lexi started to walk towards them while chewing on gum. She approached them and looked at Jimmy blowing gum then she leaned to Mia and busted it and looked at her for few seconds.

"Making new friends, huh?", Lexi asked with those serious eyes of her. Jimmy gulped seeing her like that for the first time.

"Lexi, Jimmy's Best friend", Lexi said extending her hand to Mia for a shake.

And getting Lexi's attitude Mia also accepted her hand, "Mia, Jimmy's recent friend".

That staring competition between both of the girls was making Jimmy gulp once again.

Again after weeks :

Jimmy came out while smiling brightly. Mia and Lexi were standing there waiting for him.

"Guys I got selected! Yeayyyy!", He ran to them and as Mia was already spreading her arms he went to her and hugged her first.

"Yeayy! I knew it, Congratulations!", Mia said hugging him tight.

In past few weeks Lexi and Jimmy had become good friends of Mia. Lexi and Mia were good to each other but sometimes Lexi didn't like Jimmy being too close to Mia. Like right now she was feeling the same way seeing Jimmy went to hug Mia first.

Jimmy turned to Lexi expecting a hug from her also but she just shook her hand with him.

"Congratulations buddy", Jimmy felt strange but he shrugged it.

"Ok Lexi, see you around. Let's go Jimmy we have class", Mia said dragging along Jimmy with her.

But Jimmy turned to Lexi while being dragged by Mia, "Lexi! Will have small treat after school, come on time, ok?"

Lexi smiled and showed him thumbs up.

Mia and Jimmy were in same class while Lexi was 2 years senior and Rocky was her classmate, who was her boyfriend now. Rocky loved Lexi so much but he was not good guy, always got into fight and was popular among girls because of his bad boy personality. But that's what Lexi never liked about him but she could feel his one sided love for her as she was also feeling like the same not for Rocky but someone else.

"Hey".

Someone patted on Lexi's shoulder while she was looking at Jimmy and Mia holding hands.

She turned around and saw smiling Rocky.

"Hey", She said lazily.

"Let's go for class", he said and she looked at him surprised.

"Huh? Since when are you taking classes so seriously?", She asked with raised eyebrows, he chuckled scratching back of his neck.

"I Love to attend any boring class with you", He said and she shook her head.

"Ok, wait first let me pay competition's fees for Jimmy", Lexi said and Rocky looked at her confused.

"Why are you paying for him?", Rocky asked.

Lexi pressed her lips together before saying, "He can't afford, his mom is blind and I'm his friend and I have money so why not?"

Rocky paused and smiled patting her head, "I Love You".

Whenever Lexi thought the fees was too much for Jimmy and because of that he always used to give up so Lexi always paid Jimmy's fees without his knowledge, without telling him and used to tell Jimmy that it was a scholarship which her dad had been providing to the school.

Ther friendship was so pure and full with Jimmy's innocence not until the jealousy entered.

In classroom:

"Congratulations Tolger", A boy came inside the classroom with full of sarcastic words while everyone else were congratulating Jimmy.

Jimmy's gaze turned cold seeing him. The boy was Jimmy's competitor Hiller Brone who was actually a looser but he hated to accept that because of his high ego and always tried to pick fight with Jimmy, but it never happened because of Jimmy's calm nature. Hiller cheated in many way to get selected in this audition round to represent his school but still faculty selected Jimmy and that thing pierced into Hillers ego.

And Mia knew that very well.

"A looser like you don't deserve this", Hiller said sticking his finger on Jimmy's head. Jimmy moved his hand away.

"But the looser like you exactly deserve this!", Mia interrupted sticking her finger on Hiller's head and pushed him back from Jimmy and everyone started to laugh.

"Wow! That's hot!", Hiller smirked leaning on her.

"Woah!", noise echoed in classroom.

"Eww, I can smell something's burning from you", Mia said moving away from him.

For others it was just two kids were being savage to each other but Jimmy could see the way Hiller was checking Mia out and his intensions about her. That was making Jimmy mad.

"I swear you are going love this smell, just give a chance", Hiller laughed and everyone started to whisper.

Mia gulped that was too much for her, seeing her suddenly shut Hiller smirked "What's wrong babe? Is your savage ass dreaming about m-", He was about to touch Mia.

"NO Don't! Enough! Stay in your limits Brone", Jimmy held his hand tightly which was definitely gonna leave mark.

"I'll touch her, what will you do, huh? Punch me? Beat me up?", Hiller jerked his hand and again turned to Mia who was looking down being little nervous now. Hiller again pulled her by her waist and next second, he was harshly pulled away from Mia and felt hard punch on his face giving crack to his jaw.

And the loud Gasp!

No one had ever seen Jimmy this mad. Hiller was still on the floor and he glared at Jimmy.

"I said No, Don't!", Jimmy warned again.

Hiller got up angrily, "You bloody rasc-"

"What's going on here?", Mr. Lee entered the classroom and saw Hiller was grabbing on Jimmy's collar.

"Mr. Brone! this is enough now! You are going out of control, breaking school's rules has become your habit. Let go off Jimmy right now!", Mr. Lee said but Hiller just ignored his teacher and was glaring at Jimmy.

"I said leave him or else I need to take strict actions with authorities against you", Mr. Lee warned and Hiller let Jimmy go and left the classroom while still glaring at Jimmy.

"Get back to seats students"

And everyone went to their seats but Jimmy was still looking at the door thinking about the last look Hiller gave him before going out. It was like 'You are going to pay for this'.

Mia dragged Jimmy to sit and sat beside him. Jimmy focused on lesson as Mr. Lee had started to teach but Mia was all focused on Jimmy while smiling, thinking the way he protected her, the way he stood for her.

Chapter 29

AGAIN AFTER SOMEDAYS:

"I Love You, will you be my boyfriend", Mia said looking into Jimmy's eyes, she was already nervous about Jimmy's reaction.

"W-what are y-you-"

"Jimmy, please don't say No, Take your time to think", she said making Jimmy nervous, he was not able to say anything. He didn't know how to react, he didn't want to hurt Mia.

"Mia, I-I will think", he said, she smiled.

"Thank you", She said holding his hand and leaned for a kiss. Jimmy just stared at her. Jimmy was all naive and new in these things, this was the first time someone asked him, confessing their feelings for him. But before he could process things he felt her lips on his. He blinked and moved away. She pressed her shy smile and moved back.

But then.....

"Ahem"

Their eyes widened and they both turned to the voice and saw Rocky and badly hurt Lexi.

"I thought you guys study staying late at school", Rocky said.

Jimmy gulped being all flustered and Mia was blushing mess.

"N-No actually I-I- , I mean w-we ahem.... I need to go , bye", Mia couldn't help and ran from there, Rocky laughed finding her cute.

But Lexi was on another mood, she left from there madly. Rocky frowned and followed her. Perhaps Jimmy knew the reason behind Lexi's anger.

ial*Time skipped :*

"Why did you let her?"

Seeing the bottle in her hand Jimmy got it that Lexi was not conscious. He took that bottle from her hand threw it away.

"Why did you throw that, huh?", Lexi grabbed his shirt madly.

"You should go home, wait", Jimmy said taking her phone from her and called Rocky. But before Rocky answer Lexi took that phone from Jimmy and cut the call.

Now Jimmy was mad too, he didn't know why she was taking things so personal and he wanted to talk to her but not like this when she was not even her right mind.

"What the fuck are you doing? Go home right now!", Jimmy was trying to hold her as she was not even able to stand properly.

"She kissed you here, right?", She said caressing his lip with her thumb.

She suddenly kissed him pushing him on the wall.

"What The-", Jimmy was trying to move her away without hurting her in any way physically. She was being stubborn

But somehow he managed to move her away.

"Lexi! WHAT ARE YOU DOING? Be Conscious!", He shook her.

"WHY DID YOU LET HER KISS YOU?", She was hurt, he could see it.

Jimmy somewhere knew Lexi loved him but when she accepted Rocky, Jimmy thought she was trying to move on knowing Jimmy didn't feel the same for her, he thought being his best friend she was giving him space but he was wrong. Lexi was crazily obsessed with Jimmy.

"Lexi, listen, we don't have anything between us. She just confessed me, I didn't know that she has feelings for me. I didn't even know what to say at that moment. I have not answered her yet. We are just friends", Jimmy also didn't know why he was explaining so much but for now he knew Lexi wanted to hear that only.

"Oh, so she kissed you as a friend. Ok then I'll also kiss you as a friend and I'm your best friend, it means you should give me something more", She said being drunk but that was so shocking for Jimmy. She was always desired for him. The way she was talking was making Jimmy nervous.

Lexi again wrapped her arms around him and pulled him in a kiss. Now Jimmy had enough, he was mad. He moved her away and pinned her on the wall, "I SAID STOP!"

For as second there was a pin drop silent in the middle of the unknown alley but then....

"JIMMY!"

Jimmy saw Rocky was there, Rocky went to them and released Lexi from Jimmy.

Rocky was definitely misunderstanding something because the way he threw Jimmy away from Lexi was harsh. Jimmy was hurt but he got up.

"Lexi, Are you ok?", Rocky asked worriedly checking on Lexi but Lexi started to cry.

"WHAT WERE YOU DOING?", Rocky madly asked to Jimmy.

But before Jimmy could say anything Lexi said something which was shocking for Jimmy.....

"R-Rocky..... Jimmy was f-forcing on me", Lexi said while crying.

Jimmy looked at her with wide eyes, "W-What?"

Even Rocky couldn't believe for a second but the view in front of him when he was there made him believe.

"H-He was asking for m-money, but when I denied saying I don't havem-money..... he...h-he", She hugged Rocky crying harder where Jimmy was still in shock with what she just said. He had literally stopped processing.

"How Dare You?", Rocky glared At Jimmy but Jimmy was still looking at Lexi with tears in his eyes in complete disbelief, he just wanted Lexi to lookin to his eyes for once.

"L-Lexi?", A breathy voice left from Jimmy's mouth, but suddenly he felt his collar being grabbed and a hard punch on his face. Jimmy got startled but like he didn't feel it because what Lexi did to him was more painful than the punch.

"How cheap you went Jimmy! How can you do this to your friend just for the fucking money?", he was beating Jimmy so hard that Jimmy was not even able to speak.

"N-No Rocky, I-I....I didn't d-do anything! She is lying! T-Trust me-",Jimmy was trying to say but Rocky was not letting him speak. Jimmy was helpless while Lexi was just looking at him with blank face.

Jimmy pushed Rocky. "WHY ARE YOU DOING THIS?", Jimmy yelled at Lexi, she acted scared and moved behind Rocky.

Rocky again held Jimmy and was about to hit him again but Jimmy again pushed him away crying out loud, "STAY AWAY FROM ME!"

And he left from there being all broken.

Chapter 30

Next day:

Everyone in the school was looking at Jimmy. Those whispers and things were making him weak but he shrugged because he knew he had done nothing wrong but then someone smacked his head from back.

"Woah! Boy you became more famous just by showing some guts", Hiller said and his friends laughed. "Is this your friendship?"

Jimmy got it that Rocky had told everyone in the school. Jimmy and Lexi were best friends and everyone in the school knew that very well. But this thing now shook everyone knowing that Jimmy had tried to force on his friend and now they were judging him not knowing what exactly had happened.

"Standing for one friend and harassing the other one?", Hiller was just making scene.

Jimmy glared at him, "You know nothing".

Hiller scoffed and came closer to jimmy and whispered in his ears, "And I really want to know either, it's your time to pay back Tolger and it's just the beginning". He moved back and smirked.

Hiller gasped dramatically, "GUYS THIS LOOSER IS HERE, HE SHOULD BEPUNISHED WELL! HOW SHAMELESS HE IS TO SHOW UP IN SCHOOL AFTER DOING ALL BADTHINGS TO HIS OWN FRIEND!"

"YES! HE SHOULD BE PUNISHED!"

"SHAME ON YOU JIMMY TOLGER! Such a fake friend you are!"

"Why don't you just burry yourself after doing such a horrible things?"

Suddenly Jimmy's hands started to shake, he couldn't take it and went inside the school lowering his head.

Jimmy was running in the corridor but he bumped on someone, "I'm sorry Mr. Lee".

"Umm Jimmy, I was about to call you. School authorities have removed you from representing our school in the event and your fees are returned so take note of that", Mr. Lee said, Jimmy was aging shocked.

"Why Mr. Lee?", Jimmy asked innocently not wanting to get hurt anymore.

Mr. Lee sighed, "Jimmy, whatever you have done, umm, students are against you, they don't want you present our school".

Now that's it Jimmy's tears fell. "Mr. Lee, I didn't d-do anything. Trust me", Jimmy managed to say with his cracking voice.

"I hope you are saying the truth Jimmy. Lexi's father is very disappointed with school and I think you may have to leave the school soon",Mr. Lee patted Jimmy's shoulder and left from there.

"N-no"

"Yes! He has to leave school!", Students again started to surround Jimmy again.

"Why aren't you believing me? I didn't do anything to her!", Jimmy was crying.

A boy came to him and slammed him on the locker, "THEN WHY DOES YOU OWNFRIEND IS ACUSING YOU, HUH? Lemme tell you because you took advantage of her for money! YOU CHEAP!".

Every word was stabbing Jimmy harsh, "No I-I didn't, please beli-"

But again someone pushed him on the floor and they started to bully him. Throwing trash and stuffs on him and beating him not knowing Jimmy had become numb, being sensitive how much it was affecting his mental health.

Then someone came forward moving the crowd and stood infront of Jimmy. Jimmy was blankly sitting on the floor letting them do whatever they want not having any mind state and strength to fight back. He looked up at the person who he had thought as his strength but now that person was the reason of his this state.

"J-Jimmy", It was Lexi. She could see there was only hate in his eyes for her which she had never seen before.

Lexi gulped seeing Jimmy like that, she was not able to see him like that. She was regretting. Everyone went silent seeing Lexi there. She didn't know what to do, she was drunk and hurt last night and was mad on Jimmy that's why she had said that to Rocky but now that was breaking her. But if she tellsthe truth to everyone now, they will blame her and treat her like this. She was scared to tell the truth, so looking around she didn't say anything.

"Lexi, don't forgive him. He needs to suffer", A boy said from the crowd. Her heart clenched but she was still silent.

Lexi stepped towards Jimmy but he curled himself away from her. He was so much hurt. Her one word was enough to shatter him. He was scared of her like she will again hurt him in any worse way possible.

Then,

"J-Jimmy", Mia came there and she ran to Jimmy moving people away. Tear swere falling from her eyes seeing him like that. She wiped his tears and hugged him.

"What are you all doing? Do you really think Jimmy can do something like that? Don't you know him?", She yelled at everyone and glared at Lexi.

"Why are you believing her? Have you ever seen Jimmy behaving bad with her? Not only her, he can't even imagine to hurt anyone in any way", Mia said but

"Me, I saw him last night misbehaving with Lexi. And Lexi told me that he was forcing on her because she denied to give him money", Rocky said coming out from nowhere.

"How could she? She calls herself his best friend, right?, she knows he doesn't look at any girl in bad way and wh-", Mia was saying but Rocky cut her saying , "Having innocent face doesn't mean he has innocent character too".

Jimmy was blankly staring nowhere like he was not interested in anything anymore while Lexi was looking at him.

School bell rang and everyone started to go towards their classes.

"Let's go Lexi", Rocky said and pulled Lexi from there.

"Go, I'll come", Lexi said, Rocky looked at Jimmy and again at Lexi.

"No need to talk much, come fast", Rocky said and left from there.

"Jimmy, Are you ok?", Mia asked him and helped him cleaning and dusting his clothes.

Lexi carefully held Jimmy's hand, "Jimmy....".

But Jimmy pulled away his hand and also moved away from her. Lexi knew she didn't have any right to apologize but she still said, "Jimmy, I-I'm sorry, I-I didn't m-mean-"

"Really? Then why don't you tell everyone that you lied?", Mia said.

"I-I can't …. They w-will blame me, I won-", Lexi started to cry.

Mia scoffed, "And you are expecting him to forgive you?"

"Jimmy, please say some-", Lexi said but Jimmy just started to walk from there.

"Jimmy?", Mia followed him leaving Lexi crying alone.

But someone was watching them and planning to take advantage of the situation. It was Hiller, he was watching everything with smirk, "Now the funbegins Tolger"

Chapter 31
After few days :

Today Jimmy was suspended from school because students were against Jimmy and they didn't want him in their school. School authorities still had not took any action yet but Jimmy's teacher asked him to stay at home so he'll be safe and students won't be any aggressive for any reason.

Jimmy was sitting in there silently he was not alone but Mia was with him. He had not told his mom anything as he didn't want her to worry and he was trying his best to defense himself but now it was out of his tolerance, more than his limits. Jimmy was not talking much these days, he'd been scared of people these days.

"Jimmy?", Mia handed him water but he didn't drink.

"Jimmy, drink some water".

He still didn't move, she sighed. She moved close to him and started to massage his nap to relax him little,

"Calm down Jimmy, don't stress. Everything will be fine", She said caressing his shoulder. Jimmy felt strange, he looked at her.

Her eyes were different, the way she was touching was different. She cupped his face and kissed on his lips. Jimmy was already suffering a lot and this feeling was freaking him out, he was not feeling well. He moved her away.

"W-What are you doing?", he looked at her confused.

LET ME HEAL YOU

"I'm just helping you to release your stress. I can give you whatever you want, you don't need to force anyone", she said looking into his eyes.

Jimmy gulped and moved away, "What? W-What are you saying? A-Are you also b-believing those people? Or Did you also never trust m-me?"

He was about to stand up but she held him back, "I-I... I didn't mean that Jimmy. But for now no one is trusting you, It's only me, only I can understand you then you should also understand what I want", She said with straightintention. Jimmy frowned, he understood the worst truth of the world.

No one shows love and care for you selflessly, they always want something from you. Which Jimmy's innocent soul realized late. Mia was also taking advantage of his messed mind. His broken heart was getting so many stabs at the same time.

"You are understanding, right? If you want me by your side....", With that she again kissed him and this time he kissed her back because he was finding that easy, it was kind of escape. He was out of his brain, he was becoming numb.

Suddenly they got startled with some laughter, "Hey , look here again".

Jimmy turned and saw Hiller with his boys and they were taking video of Mia and Jimmy.

"None of your business" Mia said madly.

"It is whole school's business right now", Hiller said and they again laughed.

"By the way how much is this girl paying you Tolger?", some boy asked pissing Mia more.

"Oh, does your mom teach you these seducing skills to make money", Hiller said something like this out of blue making Jimmy gulp.

And yes, he was the one who provoked other students in the school more against Jimmy.

"Huh? What do you mean?", the other boy asked.

"Don't you know? He himself is someone's dirty sin", Hiller said without any hesitation with complete intension to trigger Jimmy.

Jimmy's ears heat up, his throat dried.

"His mom was raped and she didn't even know who his father is. That's what people talk about them, who knows the truth"

"What? really? Hwaa! Tsk...Tsk....tsk....", showing fake pity they all started to laugh.

Until now Jimmy was no more, he was already strengthless and these things were making him nauseous. He was all red hanging his head low with tears in his eyes.

"Shut Up You All! Why don't you mind your own business", Mia yelled.

"Oh, so you can mind yours", They laughed.

"His mom was in that type of business I guess, that's why he knows perfect skills to make people throw their money on him", Hiller and his friends were making fun of Jimmy so insensitively.

Jimmy was dizzy, his steps made their way somewhere not knowing direction.

At Home :

"Mom", Jimmy called his mom with cracking voice.

Ella was working but she smiled hearing his voice, "Ah how's the day, mah baby?"

But he ran to her and started to cry hugging her tightly.

"Jimmy...?", she became worried.

"What's wrong? What happened? Why are you crying like this Jimmy?"

He hugged her more trying to hide in her as she was the only place he had.

"You are worrying me, say something Jimmy!", She was trying to comfort him to calm him down.

"Mom, I don't w-want to live here. Let's go from here , people are not good here, please....", He was crying drastically , Ella didn't know what to do.

"J-Jimmy, Calm down", Ella was not able to see her son but being another she could feel how desperate and scared he was.

"They are h-hurting me, I can't take this", he was acting strange, she never saw him crying and talking like this being so much affected by something and so much hurt.

Because he was expecting pure friendship but he got only pain in exchange, he had become a weak person who was not able to fight back like before. For his trust in people, he only got betrayed by them and got hurt in so worse way which was not easy to heal.

He was hating himself for not being able to fight for his mom and himself. His life was hell but the worst was yet to come.

Chapter 32

Jimmy was going home after visiting doctor as he was not well. And then he got a phone call. He saw the caller's ID and ignored; it was Lexi who was calling him. He again started to walk but his phone again rang but he kept ignoring. His phone was ringing non-stop, he checked his phone but saw Lexi's location was being shared on his phone. He frowned and answered the call.

"What do you want no-"

"J-Jimmy, help me. S-save us p-please", Hearing Lexi's terrified voice Jimmy's eyes widened.

"H-Hey, what are you saying? Where are you? Lexi?", Jimmy became worried. Even though Lexi was heartless to him but his that damn kind heart could never forget that she was his best friend once.

"Jimmy, Mia....", She started to cry.

"Lexi! What happened to her? Stop crying, tell me where are you?"

"They are d-doing bad things to h-her, they will hurt me too. H-help me please", She was crying, begging him desperately.

Jimmy's heart shook, "W-What's going o-on there?"

"I came here t-to save Mia but they beat me up Jimmy, I ran from there. They are behind me, c-come fast".

Jimmy didn't know what to do , he was already so much messed up and these things were scaring him more.

"Y-Yeah, I'm coming. Where are you?", but without thinking anything further he checked her location and turned to the direction.

"C-Come fast Jimmy, I-I'm scared"

"Yes, I'm on the way. Don-"

"Jimmy, they are here. They will hurt me, I'm no-", And suddenly call disconnected.

"Hello? Hello? Lexi?", Jimmy ran from there, his heart was racing along with his legs.

At the location :

Jimmy ran to the place where he located Lexi. But there was no one he looked around, it was alone dark alley. And then his eyes fell on something which shattered him more.

"M-Mia....?"

He went near to her unconscious figure and fell on his knees blankly. She was in miserable condition. He gulped.

"H-Hey, Wake up..... It's me Jimmy...... Mia?", He said patting on her arm with his shaking hand but he didn't get any response.

She was laying there on the ground like a trash , her clothes were torn and the way she was pale Jimmy knew what happened to her but his heart was not ready to accept it.

"I'm sorry Mia, You L-Love me, right? Ok I love-", He stopped when his eyes again caught something, he again frown taking proper look.

"Lexi?", He saw her little away from Mia in the corner. He stood up and went to her.

"Lexi....Hey see you called me, I'm here", The moment he saw Lexiun conscious he knew that he was late but his mind and heart was processing in opposite ways.

"I'm sorry, I'm late. Don't be mad like this, talk to me Lexi! C'mon wake up"

And she breathed....

Her eyes moved slowly, he patted her. "Y-Yeah, good girl. See Mia is not waking up, what happened to her? Wait, do you want water?", He was losing his mind, he was talking like a kid. It was so hard for him to go through such situation.

"J-Jimmy...."

Tears rolled down from her eyes and Jimmy was literally ignoring his tears because he was ignoring the reality.

"Wait I'll bring water for you, hmm?", he got up and went to get water for her.

And just then Rocky came there as Lexi had shared her location to Rocky also but he was not answering her calls but when he saw his phone and ran to here just to feel his world collapsing seeing Lexi there like that.

"Lexi!", He ran to her taking her in his arms, checking on her desperately.

"What h-happened to you? Who did this? Lexi!", Rocky shook her to make her conscious but Lexi was completely unconscious not aware of her surrounding and she said......

"J-Jimmy....."

His eyes widened as tears started to fill in his eyes, "Jimmy? Did he do this to you? Did he? Tell Me! Lexi! Open your eyes! Lexi! Please!". He started to cry louder.

"J-Jimmy...", and Lexi became silent.

"No Lexi!", he shook her, patted her but no response. He saw her head was bleeding, she had lots of bruises on her body. He knew what happened to her. He cried hugging her tightly.

And then he saw the other person too, "Mia?"

He went to her, "Mia? Mia?..... open your eyes look at me. Mia?" Mia was Rocky's cousin, they were not that close but they were good to each other because of their family relation. Rocky checked Mia's pulse and his heart drop knowing she was no more. Rocky carried her and was about to go to Lexi but then....

"Lexi, Here's water...", Jimmy came back with water and saw Rocky.

Rocky Put Mia down and madly stormed towards Jimmy and grabbed him harshly by his collar, "WHAT HAVE YOU DONE TO THEM?"

"I-I went to get water f-for Lexi, S-she wanted some. D-Don't worry she'll be fine", Jimmy was talking out of his mind again. But Rocky was looking at him with full anger and without any mercy he started to beat Jimmy.

"Hey! What a-are you doing? Stop! Y-you are hurting me. Please stop", Jimmy started to cry feeling pain.

"WHAT HAVE YOU DONE TO THEM? HOW CAN YOU BE SO CRUEL? PSYCHO!", Rocky was showering jimmy with hard punches letting out all of his anger.

"I-I didn't do anything R-Rocky, Lexi called me, i-I came to h-help her. N-Now they are n-not waking, I don't k-know", Jimmy was not even able to speak straight and Rocky was ignoring him.

"DID YOU REALLY REVENGE THIS WAY? YOU RASCLE!!", Rocky was beating Jimmy to death, Jimmy was scared but helpless. But Jimmy managed to push Rocky away and ran from there covering his head.

At Home :

Jimmy ran to his home and straight went inside his room and hid under his blanket just like that messily bleeding from everywhere.

"What happened Jimmy? Why are you like this?", Ella came behind Jimmy as he just ran straight to his room, she sat near him. He was so much scared, she felt his trembling body. He had high fever, Ella became so worried.

Jimmy hugged his mom tightly, "L-Lexi and Mia, They are not w-well. Something happened to them mom. But Rocky is saying I hurt them, but I d-didn't mom....I-I".

He was sounding strange, he was complaining like a kid, "Save me mom, He'll hurt me. He is not understanding, It's hurting me so much..... don't l-leave me alone please".

"Calm down baby, what are you saying? What happened to them? You are scaring me Jimmy", She was also crying not knowing what happened to him, he had been acting strange from few days and she was already worried because of that.

"Save m-me, I have d-done nothing Wrong! Trust Me!", His mental condition was worsening.

"I'm here Jimmy, nothing will happen to you my baby. Please calm down", She was caressing him.

"Don't go mom....s-stay h-her-", And his sobs faded as he lost his conscious.

Chapter 33

Next Day :

Ella opened the door, "Yes? Who is it?"

As she asked even though they were in front of her so they got it that she was blind.

"Does Jimmy Tolger live here?", A man asked.

"Y-Yes, I'm his mom. But why? Who are you?", Ella asked before letting them in.

"Cops!"

She gulped and asked nervously, "What happened o-officer?"

"We are here to arrest Jimmy under the suspect of rape and murder of Lexi Joe and Mia Charge"

Ella literally stumbled on the spot, her heart dropped. "What? No officer, you are m-misunderstanding something. He can't do s-something like this, he is innocent", She was in so disbelief.

"We'll see that madam but for now we need to take him with us. Arrest him!", He ordered his officer.

"Officer, h-he didn't do anything. Please he is sick", Ella was trying to explain to stop them but they went inside the house to check but then Jimmy came out, Jimmy was confused.

"M-Mom", he saw cops. But they started to put handcuffs on him he moved away.

"W-What's going on mom? Why are they doing t-this to me?", Jimmy tried to move away from them.

"Jimmy, t-they are saying y-you raped Lexi and Mia", Ella fell on her knees, Jimmy's eyes widened.

"W-What? No mom, I told you I have done nothing wrong. Please trust me sir! I'm-.... M-Mom tell them".

"Jimmy Tolger, You are under arrest. You have right to remain silent, anything you say can and will be used against you in court of law", And they handcuffed Jimmy.

Ella was blank, she had lost her everything. The thing she was scared of the most was happening in front of her eyes. She was crying, Jimmy went to herand held her hand.

"Mom.... I-I don't w-want to go with them, please tell them I-I have done nothing wrong......", Jimmy was pleading in front of his mom but she was not saying anything.

"M-Mom please, I'm s-scared..... Mo-"

But this time his desperation and sobs were nothing to her as she removed his hand from her. They pulled Jimmy out.

"MOM PLEASE TRUST ME! SAVE ME! I-I'M SCARED!"

.

.

"MOM!"

.

.

"MOM!"

.

.

.

.

End of Flashback (Present time) :

Jimmy's eyes were closed but tears were rolling down from his eyes. Cera was literally clutched on his shirt burying her face in his neck trying hard to control her sobs but she couldn't control any long and broke into cries.

He stroke her back still with closed eyes, "They took my mom also away from me".

"T-They kept me in custody for two years, I-I was not understanding why? But they always said it was for some investigation, t-they were still searching other culprits who they thought were with me t-that night. They were asking me about them again and again office Bern was there, somewhere he had that believe in me, he kept this matter and me away from media, there were these good people too, but you know it meant nothing to me after my own friends broke me that way, I had no hopes from others, I just kept faith in good-", Jimmy was feeling that pain same like he had felt years ago remembering those things again.

"Many b-bad things happened during that, and after 2 years they released me innocent. But my mom was still away from me. She was not like before, shed-distanced me. I-I never dared to t-ta-.....talk with her even though I was innocent. She still n-needed time to a-accept things".

"I won't blame her for anything, she had her own misery which made her hate all men and she thinks all men are same even though I'm her son. Then after an year we changed the city because people were still so interested to see and make us suffer more".

"But here, starting new life was not easy too, Rocky was still not convinced that I'm innocent because real sinners were still not caught, he found me again. He was making my life hell, he wanted me to confess my sin which I had never done. He w-was being heartless", Jimmy was hitching on breath as he was collecting himself to speak out.

But Cera was crying hard hugging him tightly, "D-Don't stop Jimmy, letit out...say it all".

"I'm tired Cera.....it's massive".

"And one day I really felt to give up, wanted to end everything so I went to bridge t-to end t-this suffer"

Cera's heart clenched more. But he chuckled in tears.

"But this Jack, he stopped me that day. I met him there, that day when I was at the end of all. But he made me understand the value of life. He told me about his miserable life and heard me out giving that shoulder to cry which I was longing for. He asked me to live little longer with him".

"He was my first friend, who loved me, helped me selflessly and you know what, I love him", Jimmy chuckled again trying to stop Cera from crying but she couldn't stop. He kissed her head.

"Don't feel bad for me Cera, now I feel so lucky and blessed to have you. I'm the happiest person", He made her to look up at him, her eyes were closed, face was wet with tears. Hiccups were giving her hard to speak. His heart was breaking seeing her like that.

"D-Don't cry Cera, I'm feeling bad. Please".

She opened her wet-swollen eye sand gulped, "J-Jimmy, try to r-remove those b-bad memories, it m-must be hurting".

Jimmy looked at her tilting his head little, he gulped looking into her eyes. He didn't know what it was but he felt like just by hearing him you were feeling his pain with that same intensity. It was hurting her in the same way.

"I'm fine Cera, as long as you are with me".

"I'm always w-with you Jimmy, Be fine. I can't s-see you like that".

Jimmy came closer to her, resting his face on her. Mixing their tears. Eyes were closed feeling each other's breath, slowly caressing each other with love.

And lips made their way on each other without knowing, sharing love and affection which was stored from long in their hearts.

"I'm sorry Jimmy, I was not there to protect you"

She thought.

"Thank you for coming to save me Cera"

He thought.

Jimmy pulled her on his lap to deepen the kiss. Leaving no gap between them they were trying to get into each other while chasing that love and finding direction to comfort each other. He laid her on the cushions and hovered her, kissing her more passionately and letting his all tears out.

But the atmosphere was heating up, he was losing himself in her completely, giving her all his love as much as he could because that was the only thing he had to give her unlimited and that's what she also wanted.

But he suddenly stopped and moved back, he looked at her closed eyes. She moved forward missing his lips but he again moved back looking at her, she opened her eyes.

"What happened?", She asked being confused.

He didn't say anything roaming his gaze all over her face.

"Don't you still trust me Jimmy?"

He caressed her cheek, "I trust you Cera, More than anyone.....More than myself".

"Then, why did you stop?"

Jimmy gulped seeing her serious and little hurt expressions. He sighed and holding her hand he kissed it.

"I'm scared that I may hurt you", he said trying to make her understand something.

"You can never hurt me Jimmy", She was talking straight looking into his eyes to assure him.

"There are many s-stuck emotions and frustration i-inside of me Cera, I won't be able to h-handle myself once I s-started to lose. And I-I don't want to let i-it out on you", Jimmy said as his eyes lowered.

But she cupped his face and made him to look at her again. "Oh, so you are going to store those things inside of you for lifetime? Killing your self every day?"

Jimmy again gulped. She caressed his soft locks.

"I don't care Jimmy, if it's going to release you from those stuck emotions and memories then go ahead because seeing you dying everyday how am I supposed to live peacefully?", Her glossy eyes were pleading Jimmy amazing him more.

"If by hurting myself I'm able to heal you then I'm ready to get hurt"

"Cera..."

"Let me heal you Jimmy", There was love and care, only love and care could be seen in her eyes which was filling his heart with lots of over whelming emotions.

He was so overwhelmed, he felt like he really found an angel by his side. No one talked with him like this ever which was giving him that confidence to live longer for her. It was so soothing to his heart.

"I Love You Jimmy", Cera said again attaching her lips to his. Jimmy's tears were falling continuously. He was sobbing in kiss. Running her fingers through his fluff hairs she was trying to comfort him.

The moment was getting intense again. Cera slightly gasped when he trailed his sweet kisses down to her neck. But Jimmy stopped again looking at her with his half-opened eyes. He suddenly carried her inside and slowly placed her on the bed and looked at her like he was filling her in his eyes. Those swollen eyes of Cera were full of confidence and trust, like she was ready to fight for him with anyone and was ready to give herself to him.

Cera smiled little, "What are you looking at?"

He smiled back moving aside that strand of wet hairs from her face, "You are so beautiful Cera".

Cera blushed on his first ever heartly compliment making him smile more. He leaned and kissed her red pink cheeks, then placing long tight kiss on her forehead he looked at his beautiful world before claiming it as his. He pecked her lips multiple times making her giggle. She started to remove his shirt, he moved back removing his shirt completely and in no time wrapping her arms around him she pulled him in a deep kiss again.

There heavy breaths and heartbeats were in race. His touches were giving her goosebumps and those tickle in tummy. He was trying his best to make her comfortable, loving her slowly yet passionately. Living the most beautiful moment of their life, they were tangled in each other letting the calm evening to be the witness.

Chapter 34

Time skipped :

Jimmy covered Cera as she was falling asleep.

"Cera....?"

She didn't answer as she was so tired and her Jimmy was getting teary for some reason.

"Hey, just t-tell me you are fine"

Cera heard his heavy voice and slowly opened her eyes half.

"Why are you crying? You have not hurt me", She chuckled embracing him.

She was not surprised how soft hearted he was, he wiped his tears, "I'm s-sorry".

"Don't cry Jimmy, I'm fine. I just want to sleep".

"Ok", moving her hairs back he kissed her forehead and fell asleep cuddling her.

At Ford mansion :

"After pushing me in the loss of billions she is having boyfriend and all?", Mr. Ford ,Cera's Dad yelled furiously.

"Boyfriend?"

"Yes Harold, leaving this luxurious life she is wondering around with some road side guy, what if someone from my friend circle or business circle sees her with him on streets like that, my all respect and status will be ruined in a snap"

Harold felt bad as Cera's Dad was still worried about his prestige and class but not Cera.

"Does she even care about anything?", Mr. Ford was frustrated.

"Uncle, I think we should give her some time. She will come back", Harold said trying to calm him down.

"Yes, this is what spoiled her, I always listen to your things and give her freedom. But not now, I want her here back as soon as possible", Mr. Ford ordered and left from there.

Harold looked down thinking about something, because he was still worried about Cera knowing she will never come back again at any cost.

Next morning :

Jimmy slipped Cera into his t-shirt while she was still in sleep, she hugged him resting her head on his shoulder to sleep more, he chuckled finding her cute. He again laid her on bed comfortably and was about to move away but she held on his shirt pulling him again on bed.

"Umm~, where are you going? Stay here", She said sleepily climbing on his chest.

"I'll go and make something for breakfast, you must be hun-", he was saying caressing her hairs.

"But I want to sleep more", She snuggled in his chest. He again chuckled seeing her acting like kid.

"Okey? You can sleep but let me g-"

"No, I want cuddles", she pouted.

He smiled and pecked her lips, she again pouted for one more, her eyes were closed.

"Don't you want to sleep now?", he said making her to open her eyes.

"Oh c'mon just spoil it, give me what I want, I'm your baby", She said pouting again and he again placed a long kiss on her lips but slightly bit on her lower lip.

She gasped dramatically looking at him, "You are being too naughty Mr. Tolger". He laughed.

But then suddenly he remembered something. He moved her on bed and got up.

"Ummhmm", She whined.

"Ayy wait", he went to cupboard to get something.

He was looking for something and finally found it, he came back to her, "This", he said showing his fist to her, she looked at it confused.

"What?"

He opened his fist and her eyes shined but with tears. She gave him a confused smiled.

It was her mom's pendant which she had given to him.

"But how? Didn't you-"

"I didn't", he smiled sitting beside her and put it on her neck.

She was so happy and confused and overwhelmed, she was not able to speak.

"This was your mom's last memory, how could I jus-"

She hugged him tightly, "Thank you Jimmy".

She moved back looking at him, "But that money? How did-"

"Don't think about that much now, just remember your all sorrows and happiness belong to me now and I promise to take care of it always", He again pulled her close to his heart.

She held that pendant and kissed it.

"Now Stop it, don't cry early in the morning. We have done that enough, now no more tears", he wiped her tears and she nodded.

At Hospital :

"Excuse me sir but it's not been 24 hours since the patient was given first dose. It will be over dose, it's not good for patient", doctor was trying to stop that man who was telling him to inject something to patient.

"You are getting your pieces, right? Then mind your business", That man said aggressively.

"But sir patient is in coma. And if I give this now, patient's life wil-"

"You Know What, I don't fucking Care", That man said with a psychic smile.

Doctor gulped and moved back, "O-Ok".

That person looked at the patient on the bed with clenched jaw.

But then Rocky entered and frowned seeing that man there, "What are you doing here?"

That man gulped looking at doctor.

"And what dose are you talking about?", Rocky asked and looked at doctor. But no one spoke.

"Hiller, what kind of dose were you talking about?", Rocky asked again seriously.

"I'll tell you", doctor said and Hiller looked at doctor shocked.

"I'm new appointed for patient and this mister is giving me money to give SPV dose to patient", doctor explained.

Hiller gulped seeing Rocky's face turning red with anger.

"He doesn't want patient to wake up soon. And the previous doctor who was in charge has been giving this doses to patient regularly from almost an year because this man bribed him to do so and that's why patient is not showing any progress", Doctor really took it risk and told the truth.

Rocky was furious, his fist clenched with red eyes, "Why are you doing this?"

He was growling in anger. Hiller gulped being scared under Rocky's dominance.

"R-Rocky…. L-Listen to m-me-"

"HOW DARE YOU!", Rocky again grabbed him harshly.

"R-Rocky, it's not me…. s-someone told me to do this! L-Leave me please", Hiller stuttered begging for his life.

"Means, You know who is behind this all, who is he? WHO IS HE?", Rocky was shaking in anger literally choking Hiller just with the grip on his collar.

Hiller was scared to death knowing if he tells the name he himself will be in trouble but it was better than being dead by Rocky.

Rocky paused looking at him….

"Don't you dare to lie! Is it Jimmy Tolger?", Rocky asked.

But

"Excuse me sir, it's hospital. Please solve your problems out", Doctor said, Rocky nodded and dragged Hiller out straight to police station.

Chapter 35

"Why are you so lazy today? Didn't you get good sleep?", Jimmy asked while carrying Cera out of the room.

"Really? You are asking me this? Whole nigh-"

"Ahem... I'm Sorry"

Cera was saying lazily closing her eyes on his shoulder but he was embarrassed.

"Hehe.... I think you sho", he stopped speaking when he saw his mom in kitchen. He gulped being nervous for some reason.

"Mom", Jimmy called her, Ella stopped for a moment and continued what she was doing. Cera's eyes shined seeing Mom after long, she got down from Jimmy and ran to her.

"Mom, I missed you. How are you?", Cera hugged her from back. Jimmy followed Cera.

Jimmy saw Ella was not reacting much, "Mom, when did y-you come?"

Ella didn't say anything, now Cera also found that strange as she was not talking anything. Cera and Jimmy looked at each other.

"Mom, I asked when did you come?"

"Yes mom, when did-"

Ella stopped again hearing them.

"When you both were busy last night", Ella replied.

Jimmy's heart dropped hearing the coldness in her voice. Cera's smile also vanished but cheeks were turning red, she moved away from her. Tears already filled in Jimmy's eyes thinking that his mom had misunderstood something.

That awkward silence.....

Cera decided to break it, "Ahem....Mom actually we were about to te-"

"Yes I'm blind but not deaf, so you better try not to fool me with your excuses", Ella said, she was sounding strange again.

Cera frowned not knowing what did she mean, but Jimmy knew what she was thinking. He held her hand, "Mom it's not wha-"

But she jerked her hand away, "Don't touch me!"

Jimmy flinched and moved away from her, tears started to fall from his eyes and Cera noticed that and said, "What happened mom? What's wrong? It's not like we have done some huge mistake, we are adults and enough mature. We los-"

"Yeah now you'll teach me, you kids these days think everything is for fun and life is joke to you all. Yes you are saying there is nothing wrong, you are adults but what if something wrong happens to you, then you'll blame him again", Ella exploded her frustration.

"No mom, you are not understanding-", Cera tried to explain but...

"And I don't want to understand, because it's late now the thing has happened which I was scared about. I was always concerned around him, telling him again and again, hurting him always but still he-.....this time I had trusted him but....", Ella was angry, she was not able to understand what Cera wanted to say.

Jimmy was just standing there looking down while holding on kitchen counter.

"And Yes mom this time also he has done nothing wrong, he has not broken your trust. He is your son. You always have taught him good things, he never forgets those, you have raised him so well and that's why people took disadvantage of his goodness. He deserves all you trust", Cera was talking trying her best to make Ella understand.

"Now also, it was not his fault. It's me..... Actually it's not even a fault..... I Love Him, We love each other. How can loving each other be fault?", Cera said, Ella was all silent listening to her.

"I'll never leave him mom, but he needs you also. He is still broken. You were always with him but he never felt that. Let him feel that you are standing by his side because he is not wrong in any way. You are his safe place and he wants you to be always. If you push him away then where will he go? And then he found that comfort in me, he wants to trust me then what's wrong in that?"

"Yeah, you were scared for something, but being behind that thing for life time don't ignore your son and his feelings. That's complete injustice with him. You also know he is all innocent", Cera's voice cracked finally and her tears started to roll down not knowing if Ella was understanding or not.

Ella was sobbing in silence too.

"I-I.... I know I have no r-right to tell you t-these things but I-I can't see him breaking alone.... I-I'm sorry", Cera left from there leaving mother and son alone there to talk. But no one was talking.

But then Ella fell on the chair while crying realizing how unfair she was with her own son.

"M-Mom...", He knelt in front of her, she hugged him.

"I'm sorry Jimmy, forgive y-your mom for leaving you alone. This darkness in front of me c-closed my mind, it took over my heart too. I couldn't see you suffering a-alone", Both broke into tears.

"Being a stranger Cera could understand you but me, your own mother failed to see your pain.... I'm so bad mother"

"No mom, Don't say like this. You are the best mom. It's not your fault, it's just my fate had these things for me. I don't care about anything but I want you", He cried hugging her tight.

"You always suffered in silence because of me, I couldn't even give you the life you deserve and just hurt you many time but you never complained", She moved him back and wiped his tears.

"But now, You found that person in your fate. Do you love Cera", Ella asked cupping his face.

"Yes mom...."

She kissed his head, "If she is the one who is destined with you then she'll never let you down. Protect her Jimmy, she needs love too".

"Yes mom, I'll always...", he smiled.

"I think I should apologize to Cera, I talked too much to her without letting her explain, call her for breakfast", Ella said and Jimmy kissed her hand and went to call Cera.

"Cera!"

Hearing him she quickly wiped her tears and turned to him.

"Yea-"

He straight ran to her and threw himself on her, Cera lost her balance and they both fell on the bed. She closed her eyes feeling his tight hug and rubbed his arm.

"Thank you Cera".

She smiled, "AHH My bones! How much are you going to break me Jimmy Tolger?

He loosened his hug and made her to sit properly on bed.

"Is everything fine?", She asked and he nodded smiling at her.

"Mom has called you", He said and her smiled started to fade.

"Is she upset with me? Is she mad?", Cera asked nervously.

"Nope!", Ella came inside gaining their attention, Jimmy helped Ella to Cera. Cera was looking down.

"I'm sorry, I shouldn't have talk-"

But Ella cupped her face and kissed her head, "No, I'm sorry my child. Thank you coming in our lives".

She hugged Cera, "You have all right to correct me Cera, My son is all yours. I have no right to call myself his mother after what I did to him-"

"No mom, don't say like this. Jimmy also won't like it, you were always best mother to him, will always be. You have your own reasons, these were just things of fate", Cera said hugging her waist.

But Ella chuckled, "In my absence, You guys have come so close that you talk same things".

Cera looked at Jimmy confused but he just smiled.

"I'm Happy for both of you, now c'mon let's eat breakfast", Ella said holding Cera's hand, Cera walked her out and Jimmy followed them.

Chapter 36

"Woah! This is so cool!", Jack exclaimed looking around Cera's new cake shop. "My first time seeing a cake shop with dark theme. By the way who was behind this concept?"

Cera smiled and pointed at Jimmy. Jimmy smiled scratching back of his neck.

"Why always bright and Unicorn concept for cakes? So I thought our dark chocolate needs their surrounding …. So yeah", Jimmy said getting Cera's wink.

"Good Job!", Jack said patting Jimmy's back.

But then Jack looked at Cera signing her something and Jimmy noticed knowing they were planning something in their evil minds but before Jimmy could say anything,

"But today we are going somewhere", Jack said glancing at Cera and she nodded.

Jimmy was still looking at them doubtfully, "Where?"

"You'll know", Cera said.

"Wait- you know?", Jimmy asked confused.

"Yes and we are going", She said Holding on his one arm and Jack held the other.

"What? But Cera this is first day of your shop and you-"

"First day is a holiday yeayy! Now let's go!", Cera and Jack dragged Jimmy out and closed the shop.

In the studio :

"Where are we?", Jimmy asked looking around but he had hint. Cera and Jack were still holding him from both of the side like he's going to run away.

"You will know, just be ready", Cera said excitedly brushing Jimmy's hairs with her fingers.

Jimmy understood that they had brought him in some kind of music recording studio, he looked at Jack, "Will anyone tell me what's going on here?"

But then someone familiar came there, "Why so late? They are waiting. C'mon let's go".

"Mike?", Jimmy was getting more confused now.

"C'mon Jimmy! Get it! Get it!", Jack said hyping his friend who seemed still clueless.

"For what?", Jimmy asked looking at all of them three.

Jack literally started to count those small lights on the ceiling to avoid Jimmy, Jimmy turned to Cera she was also looking away.

"For audition", Mike spoke.

"What?"

"Why? What happened?"

Jimmy turned to Cera, she smiled nervously.

"Actually, we brought him here without telling him anything", Cera explained to Mike while secretly glancing at Jimmy.

"Nevermind....now c'mon", Mike said but Jimmy was not ready.

Jimmy was not ready, his heart suddenly started to race, "Mike, I had told you, I don't want to-"

"But Cera told me that you are ready, that's why I have called them. They are here for you Jimmy. They have already selected Jack", Mike explained.

Jimmy looked at Jack and he nodded. Jimmy felt so happy for Jack but he stopped smiling when he realized he didn't tell him.

"There are hundreds of people waiting out for audition, but I requested them for you. So please don't waste your time. If you pass this there will be one more round but I'm sure they'll just select you. So cheer up!", Mike also didn't want Jimmy to miss this opportunity.

Jimmy looked at Cera but she looked away. Mike sighed.

"I'm giving you 10 mins, decide yourself", Mike said and went from there.

"What's going on Cera?", Jimmy asked Cera seriously but she also had enough.

"W-What? You are giving audition now! That's it!", Cera also replied seriously.

"No I'm not, I have already told you and i-"

"So what? I have forgotten that thing! You should also Jimmy".

"Cera, why are you so stubborn?", Jimmy sighed.

"Because now you are being the same", She replied not wanting him to step back this time.

"Try to understand Cera, I'm....I can't", Jimmy looked down, her eyes softened knowing his fears. "What if someone-"

"Don't think about those things for now please, your life is giving you chance Jimmy. Please go for it. I'm always here", Cera said gently holding his hand but he was not saying anything.

"Enough Now! Are you going or not?", She asked keeping her gentle side aside, he was still silent.

"Ok fine! Don't talk to me! Bye!", She said and turned to leave.

"Cera don't be childish", Jimmy said but she didn't look at him.

"Cera"

But still no. She was at the door but then she heard

"Cera", But it was Jack who had called her she turned to him.

"Cera wait- he went inside", Jack said, she smiled and came back and gave Jack high-five. Crossing her fingers she was waiting.

Inside the audition hall :

Jimmy went inside. There were two people, one was music director and other was SGT's CEO who wanted to audition Jimmy on the request to Mike.

Jimmy greeted them and stood there.

"Oh Jimmy Tolger, heard lot about you", the CEO said.

"Yeah, So are you ready Jimmy?", the director asked.

Jimmy was little flustered and seemed lost and he couldn't answer properly.

"Jimmy….?", he again called Jimmy snapping him back.

"Are you nervous? It's ok… Calm down", he said to comfort Jimmy. Jimmy nodded and looked at Mike who was standing little far from them, Mike just showed him thumbs up.

"Are you ready to sing?", He asked again.

"Yes sir".

"Do you want water?", He was trying to make Jimmy comfortable.

"No".

"Okey! Jimmy, will you go inside the record room there?"

Jimmy looked around for door and someone opened door for him and Jimmy went inside.

It was live vocal check not audition actually. As Mike had praised about Jimmy alot so they decided to check his voice on recording. He was given a headset and he stood infront of mic.

"Jimmy, what are you going to sing? Do you want music?"

Jimmy heard it in those headphones and looked out from the glass and saw it was the director who was speaking.

Jimmy gulped, "Sir, I-I'll sing a song t-that I h-had made long ago, C-Can I use t-this keyboard?".

"Oh you already song maker, good. And sure, please use it".

Jimmy smiled little.

"All the best Jimmy, Let's listen to you", He said and Jimmy again gulped looking at the mic.

Jimmy was nervous. That mic in front of him had holes which were feeling like some kind of black holes to him in which he was being pulled, like he was falling into vacuums.

Chapter 37

"He has to suffer"
"He should be punished"
"You are the worst"
"Students don't want you to represent our school"
"A looser like you don't deserve this"

He again started to hear those voices in his mind stabbing his heart, it was all in chaos. He closed his eyes taking deep breath. He started to think about positive things, he started to think about His people, His Cera.....

"Your life is giving you chance Jimmy"
"I'm always here"
"You can give better life to mom"
"This is your chance Jimmy, don't miss it"
"Mom, I'm going to be a rockstar"
"Yes Mah baby! You are a Rockstar"
"Everything will be fine...."
"Everything will be fine...."

Now these voices were calming his racing heart.

He opened his eyes and looked at the key board and slowly played a tune and he started to sing....

"More you try to go away from me,
I'll make you feel loved that more....."

"More you try to br-

But suddenly he breath hitched and he stopped. He looked up and saw them talking something to each other which he was not able to hear. He looked at Mike who looked worried too.

"It's ok Jimmy, try again', The CEO said and Jimmy nodded.

After sometime :

Cera was still crossing her fingers while waiting for Jimmy. She was nervous now not knowing what's going on inside. Rapidly tapping her feet she started to bite her nails.

Jimmy came out, she immediately stood up. But she stopped when she saw his low expressions, like he was confused with something. He came to them.

"What happened? How did it go? Was it good?", Jack started to ask him but Cera gulped. Jimmy looked at Cera.

"What? D-Did they call you for second r-round?", She asked worriedly.

"No, They didn't call me for any second round", Jimmy said still with those confused expressions.

And that's it, Cera started to blame herself somewhere. She knew now it will affect him more.

"But h-how can they? You are-"

"Because they selected me in a team with Jack", Jimmy said.

Cera's eyes widened followed by her smile.

"WHAT!", She said loudly and jumped on him hugging him tight.

"Congratulations mah Chubbs!!", She said kissing on both of his cheeks.

"But what's wrong with you? Aren't you happy", She asked giving him time.

"Yeah, I'm happy. I-I just can't believe", He smiled little making her laugh.

"I'm so happy! Yeayyy!", Cera started to jump on the spot.

"Me too", Jimmy said smiling at her happy face.

"You did it bro! Congratulations", after giving love birds their time Jack said and pulled Jimmy in a hug.

"Congratulations to you too", Jimmy hugged him back, he moved little back and looked at Jack.

"Thank you for everything Jack", Jimmy again hugged him. Jack smiled rubbing and patting his back and suddenly kissed Jimmy on cheek.

Cera gasped and pulled Jimmy away from Jack, "Hey! He is my boyfriend!".

"Before that, he is my best friend", Jack also pulled him towards him.

"NO, He is mine!", Cera again pulled Jimmy towards her.

"Oh, he is mine too. Is there your name on him?", Jack asked to tease Cera knowing her next move.

She frowned madly and pulled Jimmy's collar down to show Jack hickey on Jimmy's neck, "I have marked him".

Jimmy's eyes widened he quickly covered himself, "What The-, What are you doing Cera?"

Jack was controlling his laugh so hard, "Ok, I'll also mark him then". Jimmy's eyes again widened when Jack was literally coming to bite him. Jimmy stepped back pushing him away.

"What the fuck! Are you guys crazy? Behave!", Jimmy was so done with them and they laughed.

"You did so great Jimmy! I knew it! You are so unique and that was so amazing!", Mike said coming there and hugged Jimmy. "Congratulations".

"Thank you so much Mike, it's all because of you. Thank you for trusting me", Jimmy was so grateful of him.

"And it's because of you are so talented. Welcome to the team", Mike said and they shook hands sharing a smile.

"Congratulation to both of you, I'll inform you your schedule soon", Mike congratulated both of them for last and left from there.

"Let's go home! I can't wait to tell this good news to mom!", Cera said excitedly.

"Jack, will you go and inform mom? Me and Cera have something to do", Jimmy said holding her hand, she looked at him confused.

"Yeah Yeah, now those couple things. Your dates and all. Since you guys have started dating I'm just third wheeling I guess", Jack pouted.

"Haha no-"

"Yes, you are, why don't you find someone for yourself?", Cera said to tease him again.

"Rude-ass! I'm not interested in these dating stuffs. I'm so happy being single for now", Jack said closing his eyes with some kind of satisfaction. Cera rolled her eyes.

"Stop it you guys, Jack, will you go home?", Jimmy asked.

"Fine, have fun!", Jack said and left from there.

"Ahem... so where are we going Mr. Tolger?", Cera asked but Jimmy just smiled and dragged her out.

Chapter 38

"Wow! I have never seen this side of city. This is so beautiful, it's so cold here", Cera said rubbing her arms while feeling cold breezes. Jimmy walked near her and hugged her from behind.

He had brought her to the beautiful mountain near by the city. There were beautiful flowers, trees and the city view. Cera was admiring that view while he was admiring her.

Cera looked at him and smiled, "But why are we here?"

"You know, whenever I felt down or sad. I came here and cried my heart out, as much as I want. I cried here for hours," Jimmy was saying that with smile but Cera's smile dropped. He noticed it but continued,

"Because here is no one to judge me, no one to disturb me, no one to hurt me more. All things here always saw me crying and blaming my fate".

"But today, I want these flowers, these stones, these trees, this mountain, that sea and all things here who witnessed the weak me to know.......", He moved away from Cera.

"That how happy I'm! how blessed I'm! and how loud I can laugh now!", He said loudly making Cera chuckle.

"Because now...... I have YOU!", He pointed at her.

"YOU Cera! You are everything that I want in my life!", His eyes were glittering with happy tears.

"I LOVE YOU CERA!"

"I Love You So Much!"

That's the first time he confessed out loud spreading his arms. Cera didn't want to cry at that moment because she was happy but she couldn't stop her tears. Jimmy fell on his knees in front of her still spreading his arms.

"I love you", he let out a breath of relief feeling so light after confessing what's in his heart and how true it was.

Cera's heart was racing on the highest speed and those butterflies were literally having party in her stomach to tease her more. She was so overwhelmed seeing the love of her life was confessing her there in front of her, getting on his knees. She walked near him and he stood up, she wiped his tears.

"You are mine", he smiled cupping her face and wiped her tears, she smiled back and nodded.

"I love you too Jimmy"

He held her hand resting his forehead on her. They closed eyes while tears were still rolling down from both of their eyes.

"Thank you for pulling me into life again. You are my guardian angel Cera".

She chuckled and opened her eyes and saw his closed eyes but he still had that smile.

"Thank you for trying.... For us", she said and he opened his eyes. He kissed her head. She moved away from him.

"This is really so calm here", she said walking around but he held her wrist and again pulled her close.

He was looking into her eyes asking her for something, he was so close to her with different teasing smile making her heart go crazy, she looked at him with 'what?' look.

"I have not got my answer yet", He said wrapping his arm around her waist.

"Huh-? I have already said, I love you", she said being confused.

"I didn't get it in your way", he said glancing at her lips and leaned to kiss her but she stopped him and looked at him with raised eyebrow to tease him. He looked away to hide his blushing face, only he knew how much courage he had collected to ask for a kiss.

She chuckled finding that cute. She wrapped her arms around his neck, "You want answer, right? Then tell me what can you do for me?".

"Whatever you say", he said with full confidence.

"Ok, umm, Jump off that cliff", She said pointing at the edge of the mountain. His expressions fell, he looked at her in disbelief. She started to laugh hard moving away from him, finding his expression drop funny. He smiled shaking his head.

"Jimmy, I was jus-"

Suddenly he started to step back, her laugh started to fade.

"Jimmy?"

He was smiling at her and suddenly started to run towards the cliff confusing her. But her eyes widened, "N-No JIMMY!"

Her legs became weak when she realized what he was going to do but she snapped herself back and ran behind him.

He was running all the way, there a single slip and it was end.

"JIMMY stop! What the hell are you doing?"

But seemed like he couldn't hear her. He was going near to edge. Cera stopped and took deep breath and....

"JIMMY! STOP!"

And Jimmy stopped and turned to look at her with the same smile. And here Cera was panting with pounding heart. She pushed her hairs back gasping for air but felling relieved. She again ran to him.

He opened his arms to embrace her, she threw herself in his arms and started to cry.

"Are y-you crazy? What do you think you were doing? Why did you do that?", She was crying hard.

"Because I knew you'll stop me", He could feel her beating heart near his.

"I was j-just joking", Cera was trembling in his arms.

"But I was not, I was proving my love", He said, she moved him away and slapped on his shoulder.

"No need to prove anything, I-I know you love me. Y-You scared me", She said trying to calm herself.

"Haha, I'm sorry".

"Think before doing anything stupid. You are Crazy".

"Yeah, CRAZY IN LOE WITH YOU", he again said loudly lifting her up little and she laughed in tears.

Sniffing cutely, she pecked his lips but he again pulled her in a kiss, she smiled kissing him back.

Time skipped :

It was already evening, Jimmy and Cera were walking towards home.

"Will you be away from me for few months?", Cera asked pouting while hugging his arm.

"Umm, Nope! Let's not talk about it for now, we still have time", Jimmy said caressing her hand.

"But Jimmy, I always get bad feeling whenever I feel so much happy. I'm happy today but I'm scared too", She said thinking about something. He stopped and turned to her, it was second time he was hearing this from her and she had that same worry in her eyes.

"Hey, these are just your thoughts. Nothing will happen, don't overthink everything will be fine", He said gently holding her hand. She smiled on the way he was talking so sweetly and with so much care.

"Do you think so?", She asked and he nodded.

"Ok then", she chuckled and hugged his arm again and started to walk but suddenly they heard loud honk. And as soon as Cera looked behind a car was racing toward them and was so close. Jimmy was out side to the road her eyes widened when she realized it was about to hit Jimmy,

"Jimmy!"

Cera pulled Jimmy inside to the walkway so hard that they both fell on the ground and the car passed by them with full speed from an inch away.

"What the heck!", Jimmy looked at the car in disbelief.

"Are you ok Cera?"

She nodded but saw Jimmy's elbow was scratched.

"You are hurt", She checked him worriedly.

"It's ok let's go home", He said helping her to stand up but Cera looked at the car doubtfully.

That car belonged to her father's men.

But she didn't say anything. The way she was feeling careless after hearing his sweets talks few mins ago, now she was more scared than that for some reason.

"Hey, are you hurt?", He asked finding her lost.

"No, I'm fine. Let's go and treat you", She said and they walked toward home holding hands again.

Chapter 39

Jimmy and Cera came home after having great time, but their smile dropped. They both stopped, Ella and Jack were there but few other people caught their attention.

"C-Cops?", Cera looked at jack confused.

"Mr. Tolger, we want you to come with us", One of the officer said.

"W-Why?", Cera asked holding Jimmy's hand.

Jimmy's palm started to sweat, he gulped.

"I can't share any information with anyone for now Miss but don't worry, Myself officer Reid. I was with Mr. Tolger for two years and I was the one who helped him prove his innocence. He'll come back soon, I'll personally come to drop him. He won't be in any trouble so don't worry. Please cooperate", He said and put his hand on Jimmy's shoulder, Jimmy looked up and nodded.

"I'll also come", Cera said not wanting to leave Jimmy alone.

"No! not y-you", Jimmy immediately refused, because he didn't want her to see him there if something bad happens there, he didn't want her to see him weak anymore.

"But I won't let you go alone", Cera said holding his hand tighter.

"I.... I will go with him, may I also come officer?", Jack asked.

"Fine", officer said and with that they turned to leave but Cera was not letting go of Jimmy's hand.

Cera was not feeling well, that bad feeling like if she let him go she won't be able to see him again was making her sick. Her heart was not allowing her to let his hand go, it was beating with that bad feeling taking over it.

Jimmy turned to her and saw her teary eyes.

"Come b-back soon", Cera said but her voice cracked.

"I will, don't worry", Jimmy said slowly removing her hand from his and she suddenly felt so empty, like something in her was telling her to hold him tightly again feeling unsafe without him.

And they all left from there. Cera closed the door and turned to Ella who was all silent this whole time.

"Don't worry mom, he'll come back soon. Jack is with him", Cera said to assure her. But she didn't know if she was assuring Ella or herself.

"Yeah", Ella said but she was still worried.

At police station:

"Jimmy, not really good to see you here again but I just wanted you to know we have found real culprits because of whom you had to suffer, Your friend's sinners. That's why I called you here to let you know", the officer who was sitting on his chair said as soon as Jimmy and Jack entered.

This was officer Bern, Officer Reid and Officer Bern were with Jimmy during those tough two years. They helped Jimmy lot, they were trying their best to prove Jimmy was innocent because somewhere they found that innocence in his eyes or by talking with him. They were also the reason of Jimmy at least believed that good people still exist even though he knew at that time that he was not in state to trust anyone.

Hearing officer Bern Jimmy just nodded because he wanted to move on, he knew it was going to hurt him more.

"Bring them", Officer Bern ordered.

And two officers dragged Hiller inside followed by Rocky. Jimmy saw Hiller and also recognized him even after 7 years but he was not surprised at all. Jimmy was trying to forget everything; he was not even interested to see who was this real culprit. He just wanted to run away from all those thoughts but the situation was making it hard for him.

"Jimmy, do you know him?", Officer Bern asked.

Rocky was looking at Jimmy as he was only looking down.

"Hiller Brone", Jimmy said looking up.

"Then you also know Mr. Rocky, don't you?", Officer Bern again asked. Jimmy just nodded.

"Hmm, By the way Mr. Rocky is the one who found the real culprit not only this guy Hiller but there is someone else too. Bring Him!", He again ordered.

And again someone was being dragged inside, they were surprised seeing the person even Jack was surprised.

"Isn't he the guy who always comes with Rocky? What's his name?", Jack thought for his name.

"S-Sonki", Jimmy said in broken words.

"Yes, Mr. Rocky's friend", Officer said and they made Hiller and Sonki knelt there infront of officer bern.

"So now, Mr. Sonki is going to tell us why he did want to do that brutal act, ok? Everyone take seats please", Officer Bern said tapping his stick in his palm. They were hanging their head low without saying anything.

"Will you tell or shall I make you speak?", Officer glared at Sonki.

"B-Because of this Tolger! Yes Him! He was the worst part of my diary! Which I wanted to tore off and I did", Sonki spoke with rage.

"He was all perfect even though he was poor fellow. My dad always used to praise him in front of me! Always compared me with him when we were in school. I was so pissed, I wanted to get rid of him from my life".

"Rocky was my friend, I told this to him but he never took it seriously because Tolger was his girlfriend's best friend. Rocky always shrugged it taking his side. So one day I met Hiller who was in same problem as me. He asked him for help"

"I sent my girlfriend Mia to spy Tolger and destroy him but he played with her too, that idiot Mia really fell in so called love with him. But suddenly something happened and whole school went againt Tolger, so taking the chance I was about to do something but Mia came in my way. I knew Tolger was going crazy, he was mentally sick. I was planning to provoke Tolger to end himself that night but Mia got to know about it she tried to stop me"

"I was so mad on her that day, I forced on her that day but don't know how she died. I didn't mean to kill her but that Lexi also come there out from no where and saw me with Mia and started to say that I killed Mia and ran from there I knew she'll tell everyone so I sent my men behind her. They beat her to death a-and I d-don't know w-what else they did to her, I don't know how.....h-how.....How she survived.....?", Sonki was talking like crazy person , like some maniac.

Rocky's fist and jaw clenched and tears were falling from his eyes.

"I blamed that on Tolger, I called Rocky and told him that Tolger was there with Lexy and Mia. All these years I was with Rocky filling all bad things about Tolger in his mind. But Rocky again started to investigate after all these years. Who does he think he is?", Sonki glared at Rocky while crying and his psycho side was coming out.

"He is crazy behind that Lexi! But she is in coma. I tried my best to keep her in that sleep forever but this Hiller fucked up!", Sonki hissed at Hiller madly.

"Jimmy!", Jack held Jimmy as he was about to fall.

"Jimmy, are you ok?", Jack asked worriedly as Jimmy was looking at him with half open eyes and was not breathing properly, he had blank expressions but tears were continuously falling from his red eyes. Jimmy was feeling to throw up, it's was so suffocating with that lump in his throat. But someone was watching him with pitiful eyes feeling guilty and that was Rocky.

"Jimmy, Are you alright? Bring water", Officer Reid told someone while checking on Jimmy. He knew Jimmy for 2 years, he had seen his pain and the way he suffered. And he knew that Jimmy was not mentally strong to take anything more.

"Calm down... calm down Jimmy", Jack was continuously rubbing his back.

"I w-want to go h-home", Jimmy uttered being half conscious. Jack nodded and looked at Officer Bern for permission.

"Yeah, take care", Officer said and Jack helped Jimmy to get out from there.

Chapter 40

"Are you feeling better?", Jack asked handing Jimmy a cold drink.

"Hmm", Jimmy simply replied.

"Why do you think so much and stress yourself? Didn't I tell you to try to live carelessly? If you care over small and unnecessary shits it will stress you more which is complete nonsense", Jack said hoping he was understanding.

"I-I..... I couldn't s-save them Jack", Jimmy said out of blue. He turned to Jack and Jack pulled him in a hug.

"And I c-can't throw it out from my mind, it's going to be there somewhere with me for lifetime. All happened because o-of me Jack".

Jack had thought Jimmy was crying because these many years he was being punished for someone else's sins, but he was actually crying because he was not able to save his friends in past. And now was blaming himself for it.

"Hey, what are you saying, huh? Don't get these things in your mind, it will be harder for you", Jack could understand as Jimmy had the most kind and fragile heart. He just caressed his back to calm him as he was still trembling little.

"Jack, I was the-"

"J-Jimmy....?"

They turned to the voice and saw Rocky. They stood up and Jimmy was about leave but....

"Jimmy, please can we talk?", Rocky asked as gently as possible. Jimmy stopped but didn't turn to him. No one was saying anything. Jack could see how much Jimmy was controlling himself. And Rocky didn't know how to start.

"Hey.... Lexi isn'-", But as Rocky started

"Rocky, let's talk some other day but not now. I hope you'll understand", Jack said calmly, he knew he should not pull his aggressive form for now as Rocky was there just to have simple talk. But he also knew Jimmy was not in state to have any talk.

Jack said and left from there with Jimmy. Rocky sighed looking at them going from there.

After sometime at home :

Jimmy and Jack came back to home. And as soon as Ella felt their presence she got up from couch.

"Jimmy...?"

"Yes mom", He replied.

"What happened there?", She asked.

"N-Nothing, everything is fine mom. Don't worry", Jimmy said hugging his mom feeling safe again. But he moved back.

"Where is Cera?", Jimmy asked and she gulped, Jimmy caught her worry.

"What happened mom? Where is Cera?", Jack asked as she was not answering.

"Cera!", Jimmy called her but didn't get any reply. Jimmy looked at Jack confused.

"Jimmy, C-Cera......", Ella was nervous.

"Cera? What happened to Cera? Is she fine?", Jimmy asked being worried.

Ella took breath, "Yea s-she is fine....but After you left Harold had come and...... he took her with him".

"What?", Jimmy looked at Jack.

"What? But why? Didn't you stop him?", Jack asked as he was worried too.

"Yes, I did even Cera didn't want to go but he took her forcefully saying her dad wants her there right now. And told you n-not to contact her. I-I'm sorry Jimmy", Ella was feeling bad as she was no help.

Jack looked at Jimmy who was in some kind of deep thought.

"What? Really? Wait- let me call her", Jack said but,

"You can't talk with her, she left her phone here", Ella said and Jack saw her phone on couch.

"Ok, I'll call Harold", Jack was about to call him but Jimmy stopped him.

"Jack, it's ok. He is her brother, he knows what's good for her.", Jimmy sounded serious.

"But there is nothing good for her Jimmy, You don't know her dad. He'll cage her again", But Jack was worried.

"I know and I'll go to meet her soon and bring her back", Jimmy said and left from there. Jack was looking at him speechless because he was so confident like few minutes ago he was crying mess and now was like main lead he announced his commitment. He had some different kind of energy when things came to his Cera.

"What was that?", Ella was as speechless as Jack. Jack chuckled.

"Was that Jimmy?", She was shocked too.

"Yeah", Jack laughed.

"She has completely changed him, I'm so proud of him", Ella was happy.

"Me too", They laughed as they were relieved after what Jimmy said.

"Ok, I'll leave now and try to talk with Harold", Jack said.

"Ok, take care".

And Jack left.

Jimmy was thinking about how to bring Cera back, he was thinking about all the possibilities of consequences if he goes right now to her house, but getting thought of your dad and his man he decided to wait as Harold had also told him not to contact Cera for now. It was not like he was scared of her dad or something but he knew in hurry things can mess up. But he was worried about her. He knew she never wanted to go back there, her crying face was making him restless.

Her words started to echo in his mind

"But Jimmy, I always get bad feeling whenever I feel so much happy. I'm happy today but I'm scared too"

"I'll make everything right. Nothing will happen", He talked to himself.

He had decided not to be weak, now it's his turn for his love, for his Cera he was ready to fight with world. He wanted her back. This time he didn't break down but tried to build more confidence and strength.

"Don't worry my love, I'll come soon".

"Jimmy?"

Jimmy saw his mom standing on the door, she walked in and he helped her and made her sit on the bed and he laid on bed resting his head on her lap.

"Already missing Cera?", She smiled caressing his hairs.

"Nope, She is always here", He replied putting her hand on his chest.

She chuckled, "Ehee, Since when you became like this?"

"Since she has come in my life", He again replied with smile. She patted his cheek.

"What if her dad doesn't let you meet her or let her come with you?", She asked little worried.

"Mom, ok, I'll tell you but don't tell anyone"

"Okey...?"

"I'll steal her from there", He slowly whispered and they laughed.

Jimmy could see his mom was worried, he just wanted to light her mood.

"Don't worry mom, one day I needed to talk with her dad so that the one day has come. I'll talk with her dad and if he is ready to let her go with me then that's fine and if he doesn't allow her then also I don't care with his decision as long as Cera wants to be with me"

Ella smiled hearing his son so confident and cheerful after so long. He got up and hugged her.

"Don't worry I'll bring your daughter in law soon", He said.

"Daughter in law? She is my baby", Ella said.

Jimmy pouted, "No I'm your baby".

He kissed her cheek like a kid. She again laughed.

Chapter 41

NEXT MORNING AT FORD MANSION

:

Cera slowly opened her eyes feeling pain in her back and neck and realized that she was sleeping just like that in sitting position while hugging her knees after crying whole night.

She was in her house which was not feeling her home anymore, she still wanted to go home. She found herself in her huge room which was like a cage to her. She just wanted this to be a nightmare, she just wanted to fall asleep and woke up in Jimmy's arms. She again started to cry. She weakly got up from bed and went to door but door was locked.

"Is t-there anyone? P-please open the door....", She cried but no one heard.

"I won't run away, please... u-uncle Shawn? Are y-you there?", Cera started to bang on door.

"OPEN THE DOOR! I'M NOR LIKING IN HERE!! Please", She rested her head on the door and slid down while crying hard.

"I'll die here, please let me out". Cera was able to live without food or water but she couldn't stand a minute without freedom. That's what her biggest fear was. She wanted to go out from there.

She got up wiping her tears, "I-I.... I'll jump out of the w-window! I'm warning y-you! I'll jump!".

LET ME HEAL YOU 175

She went to window and opened it and was about to get on it but someone opened the door and stormed to her and pulled her away from the window.

"Cera! Are you crazy? It's 5th floor", Harold Pulled her away and closed the window.

"WHY DO YOU CARE? GO AWAY!", Cera pushed him away harshly. "HOW CAN YOU DO THIS TO ME?", Cera was screaming frustratedly.

"I-I was happy living my life with Jimmy, how can y-you just ruin it like t-that? I trusted you", She again fell on her knees while crying, Harold was feeling bad but he couldn't go against Mr. Ford.

"I love Jimmy", Cera said.

"Then forget him!"

Suddenly that stern voice hammered on Cera's ear making her madder. Cera glared at her dad.

"Forget about him, because you are going to marry Mr. Roger's son", Mr. Ford said coldly without being bothered by his daughter's condition.

"Don't tell me what to do! I will not marry anyone", Cera was furious and tears were still falling from her eyes.

"I love Jimmy and I'll only marry him! You Better Get It! AND LET ME GO FROM HERE! YOU CAN'T DO THIS".

Mr. Ford's jaw clenched he madly walked to her but

"Uncle, calm down. She'll do!", Harold said trying to calm him.

"No, I won't! I'll kill myself!", But Cera had different plans.

"Don't talk crazy Cera", Harold scolded her.

"Yeah, sure do whatever you want but after marrige where I want!", Mr. Ford was also with his stern decision.

"Is this what he taught you? Yeah, you got guts I see. You have become more stubborn. Being brat again Cera...? But I know how to bring you back on your place", Mr. Ford said crouching to her.

"Last night they just missed by inches, didn't they?", He said, making Cera stop crying and she blinked as weird nervous feeling started to took over her.

"W-What are you s-saying?"

"You protected him from getting hit last night, right?", He was talking so casually. But Cera's eyes widened realizing something.

"N-No...", Cera was looking at him in a complete disbelief.

"But now you are here, I wonder who will protect him?", Mr. Ford smirked.

"Y-You can't.... You are so bad Dad", She again cried helplessly.

"Then you need punishment for acting brat".

Mr. Ford grabbed on her arm and made her stand and started to drag her somewhere.

"N-No where ar- No, Not there dad! No please! Leave me! Harold say something", Cera's anger was replaced with some kind of fear. She was begging him to stop.

Mr. Ford was taking her to lock in a dark room, he always punished Cera like that and that became her childhood trauma, being locked in a dark room was the most scary thing for her.

"Uncle, relax, she won't do it again", Harold tried to talk with Mr. Ford.

"No! not today Harold! She has embarrassed me enough! She needs lesson!", Mr. Ford just glared at Harold as he was not in not mood.

"No dad! I don't like there! Please DON'T!", Cera screamed pushing him away.

"No Please leave me alone!", she cried hiding behind Harold.

"You are doing this all for that boy, right? Ok then, I'll just end his chapter", Mr. Ford had trapped Cera from both sides.

"NO! Please don't hurt him! Why are you doing this to me?", She again begged him to stop but

"Now you, don't tell me what to do!", Mr. Ford said and started to walk out.

"NO DAD! STOP I'LL DO WHATEVER YOU SAY! PLEASE STOP!", Cera again screamed falling on her knees infront of her father but couldn't budge his heart.

He stopped and smirked looking at his daughter crying drastically.

Cera was so scared and trembling just by the thought of Jimmy getting hurt because of her and in fear of being locked in dark room.

"Good Girl! You should know your place honey, I wouldn't have gone this harsh on you", Her dad again knelt infront of her and caressed her head.

"Now just like a good girl as you are and forget about your that boy and be ready to get married", He held her hand and made her to stand and then made her sit on the bed. He paused looking at her.

"And one more thing, Don't try to do anything stupid or hurt yourself. I know you love that boy and now you know what I can do. Here your one crazy act and there his life will destroy in a snap", He said gently stroking her hairs.

"P-Please don't hurt him, he is innocent. I'll do w-whatever you say dad, I won't try to run away please stay away from h-him", Cera was still pleading while holding on her breaking heart.

"Yes, and for that you need to stay away from him".

Cera nodded rapidly like her life depends on it.

"Good, see how obedient you are but sometime becomes so stubborn. Now eat something like a good girl", He said sweetly patting her cheek and left from there after shattering her completely.

Cera again started to cry louder, Harold was feeling so bad seeing Cera like that, "Cera I'm sor-"

"Please leave...."

Harold sighed and went out. She again hugged her knees crying silently.

"Help me Jimmy, p-please take me out from here", She closed her eyes and tears fell.

Chapter 42

"I'm telling you to call your Boss, I have something important to talk with him", Jimmy said to the guards who were stopping him from going inside the Ford's Mansion.

"Our boss is busy he doesn't have time to talk with you. You need to take appointment", one of the guards said trying to stop Jimmy from going in.

"But it's not a business proposal to make an appointment, I want to talk to him about our relation", Jimmy replied simply yet confidently but they started to laugh.

"Just leave already boy, you are wasting our time Mr. Ford don't meet anyone without appointment", Manager said.

"Why would I need appointment when I'm his future son in law, tell him Cera's boyfriend is here", Jimmy said smiling.

Manager's eyes widened, "Hey! What are you talking about, huh? Leave from here". They started to push Jimmy out.

"Hey don't push me. I'll meet Mr. Ford", Jimmy started to insist moving them away.

"Jimmy....?"

Jimmy heard a familiar voice and he smiled, "Harold".

"What are you doing here?", Harold asked seeing Jimmy being held by guards.

"Harold, why did you take Cera back without telling me, huh? I was worried, you had promised her that you won't tell her dad, then? Where is she? I'm here to take her back", Jimmy said still struggling with guards. Harold sighed and signed guards to let Jimmy go. Jimmy immediately went to Harold.

"I love Cera... W-We love each other", Jimmy said with that confident smile again making Harold confused with his changed behavior.

Harold sighed again, "No you can't take her from here".

"Huh- Why?", Jimmy asked raising his eyebrows like he really didn't know anything, like he really didn't care about anything. Harold was surprised as Jimmy was being too casual.

"What do you mean 'Why?'? Her dad won't allow her", Harold replied but lowkey he was curious about Jimmy's next words.

"Whatever, I don't care. She is my girlfriend and I know she also don't like to stay her. So I better take her out from here. And her dad can't stop me", Jimmy literally smirked.

"But what if she denies to come with you?"

They heard voice from behind it was Mr. Ford, he walked towards them.

"Why would she? She loves me and her safe place is me. She doesn't feel good here, I know very well. By the way I'm Jimmy Tolger, Cera's boyfriend, Hi! Nice to meet you Mr. Ford", Jimmy said giving a gentleman smile with bow as he guessed it was Cera's Dad by his attire and attitude.

Mr. Ford raised his eyebrows seeing the young man's gut calling himself his daughter's boyfriend.

"Seems like you know her more than me", Mr. Ford said.

"Definitely!", Jimmy said without any hesitation. "Of course I know her better than you! I have talked to her more than you have done ever, I have understood her completely which you have never done in years", Jimmy was talking those offensive things very sweetly.

Harold was already surprised because he only knew Jimmy as a silent introvert boy who doesn't like to get into fights. Mr. Ford found Jimmy little challenging but he stayed calm to see how far Jimmy can go.

Mr. Ford wasn't saying anything but just looking at him coldly, Jimmy sighed. "Where is Cera? I want to meet her", he said, more like demanded to have his girl in front of him right now.

Mr. Ford sucked on his cheeks looking at Jimmy.

"Harold, will you please call my lovely daughter?", Mr. Ford said surprising Harold more. He was not understanding what was happening. He just gulped and nodded and went to bring Cera. Meanwhile Jimmy and Mr. Ford were having a cold stares competition.

After sometime Cera came down with Harold. Jimmy smiled.

"Cera".

But Cera didn't look at him.

"Cera....?"

"Yes dad?"

"Come her sweetheart", her dad called her so she went to him.

"See someone is here to meet you", Mr. Ford said but she didn't look up because she knew if she looks up at Jimmy her tears will fall.

"Look at this Mister dear, do you know him? He is calling himself your boyfriend", Mr. Ford left no option for her but look up.

She slowly looked up at Jimmy blankly who was smiling at her but she again turned to her dad and.....

"No Dad, I don't know him", Cera simply replied like she had been taught to say only that. Mr. Ford smirked.

Jimmy's smile dropped, he looked at Cera being confused, "What are you saying Cera? I'm here to take you with me, I know you don't-".

"That's it now Enough! She said she doesn't know you. Now you can't force my daughter for anything. Cera, go inside", Mr. Ford ordered.

Cera's eyes met with Jimmy's and he understood everything seeing tears in her eyes. His heart ached her eyes were begging for help but still wanted him to leave from there. She turned away and started to walk from there.

"Cera... Look at me, Cera...", Jimmy called her but she didn't stop and just closed her eyes while walking.

"Security! Take him out!", Mr. Ford ordered and two guard held Jimmy but he jerked away.

"Dare. To. Touch. Me. Again!", Jimmy gave them a sharp gaze making them gulp.

Jimmy looked at the direction Cera left and smiled sadly.

"Don't worry my love, I'll come back again. I LOVE YOU! MWAHHH!", Jimmy said loudly to let Cera hear and she definitely heard.

Jimmy smirked at Mr. Ford just to annoy him more and left from there.

And on the other hand Cera was crying mess.

"I'm sorry Jimmy".

But his words were recalling in her mind.

"Don't worry my love, I'll come back again. I LOVE YOU!"

"N-No..."

Suddenly she became scared thinking her dad might try to hurt him again.

"I need to stop Jimmy", She got up but she had nothing to contact with him.

And this time Cera didn't want to take any risk by taking help from Harold. She sat on the bed while thinking forgetting her state she was worried for Jimmy. While she was in thoughts someone entered.

"Cera baby, Lunch for you", It was uncle Shwan one of their servants and Cera's caretaker.

"I don't want to eat uncle Shwan", She replied lazily.

"Baby, you have not eaten from last night. Eat something", he said trying to convince her.

Cera suddenly started to cry not knowing what to do.

"Oh my- don't cry Cera. You also know how your dad is", He said gently caressing her head.

Uncle Shwan had been looking after Cera and taking care of her since she was 10 years old but he also couldn't go against your dad as he was just a servant.

"But w-why uncle? Why is he like this? Why doesn't he understand me?"

"I'm sorry Cera baby, I can'-" Suddenly his phone rang and he answered and just then Cera's mind lightened up.

He went little away from her to talk. Cera decided to ask him for help. After talking on phone when he come back, Cera stood up.

"Uncle, I need your help please", she pleaded.

Chapter 43

Jimmy was walking back and forth while rubbing his temple. He didn't know what to do further, because they were not allowing him near to mansion. And Jimmy knew Cera needed help, he couldn't let her be like that, he was not able to stay calm at this situation. Cera's helpless image was not leaving his mind, her pleading eyes for help was making him impatient.

"Harold is also not answering my calls, what's wrong with him?", Jack said being worried because he also understood that this time Cera's dad was being too much.

"Mom, She didn't even talk to me, she was just crying. How can I help her? I don't even know if she is fine", Jimmy was so restless.

"Calm down Jimmy, we'll find a way", Ella tried to calm him.

Jimmy sat on the couch desperately tapping his feet not able to find any way. They had idea of informing cops but Jack knew Cera's dad, that idea wouldn't have worked he knew.

While they were thinking, Jimmy and Jack both received some notification on phone. They checked their phone and looked at each other, it was from Mike as he had sent their Routine schedule from day after tomorrow.

"I'll talk with Mike later", Jack said and Jimmy nodded.

But Jack's phone again beeped he saw it was some voice message from unknown number so he just ignored swiping it away but instead he accidently opened it and......

"Jimmy, I'm sorry. But please-"

They heard Cera, Jimmy looked at phone and then at Jack.

"It's voice message", Jack said and replayed. Jimmy took phone from him.

Audio message from Cera : "Jimmy, I'm sorry. But please don't come here again. He'll hurt you. Don't worry about me, I'm fine. I know your schedule will start soon, please focus on that for now. I know you'll come to take me but please not now. And Jack, don't talk with Harold he'll spoil everything again. This is uncle Shwan's phone, I'll send voice messages like this again. Don't call or text on this number, ok?"

"Tell mom also that I'm fine here and not to worry. And good luck to both of you for your new journey, now stop worrying about me and work hard!"

"I'm fine Jimmy.... Please don't worry".

Message ended.

"She is not fine", Jimmy said as tears fell from his eyes.

"But I think you should do what she said. And she said she'll send message again, ok? Don't be so down, Cera is smarter than you", Jack said putting hand on his shoulder.

"He is right Jimmy, Cera doesn't want you to be weak because of her", Ella said patting his back.

Jimmy nodded, "Yes, yes mom. I will not be weak anymore. We are going for training".

Jack smiled proudly and patted his back.

After 5 days :

Jack and Jimmy were dance practicing. They had made a team which was trio for now and members were Jack, Jimmy and Mike. Jimmy and both were asked if they want to go solo or being a group, and they both gladly chose to be in group and Mike also decided to go with them as they had become good friends. But they needed two more members but audition was going on. But they had to start their training any how as they were going to debut as a group next year and they needed at least an year to be trained well with their skills.

But for now, it was just Jack and Jimmy were dancing in front of huge mirror in the hall. But Jack noticed Jimmy was not focused as he was messing most simple moves. Jack stopped and turned the music off but Jimmy didn't even realized that music had stopped as he was still dancing without music and when he realized it, he found Jack looking at him. Jimmy sighed looking away. Jack knew Jimmy was not able to concentrate because Cera had not sent any message yesterday and he was waiting for it.

"Did you get it?", Jimmy again asked and Jack shook his head.

Cera was only sending message on Jack's phone because she only knew his cell phone number.

During these days Jimmy had been secretly sending Cera letters with flowers to let her know that he's receiving her messages and to tell her that he was also fine. But yesterday he didn't receive any message from her so he was bit worried.

"She must be not get- Owk- here you go!", Jack smiled brightly looking at his phone and Jimmy got it that it was message from Cera. He quickly took phone from him and played it.

Audio message from Cera : "Hehe, missed me? I'm sorry I couldn't message yesterday. Anyways how's my Bear doing? I hope everything is fine. Here also everything is fine. Just..... Missing you a lot".

"And received your flowers yesterday, Uncle Shawn secretly received for me. Thank you for the flowers, I felt so special. Doesn't it feel like a perfect love story now? *chuckles* Have you eaten? I did, don't worry. Don't over work! Hey Jack! you better take care of my Bear or else I'll kick your ass. And also take care of yourself, I don't want to say it but I'm missing you buddy"

"And Mom, I'm missing you too. You must be alone at home without these guys. Please take care.... Ummm that's it I guess, bye".

Ended.

Jimmy sighed and leaned back on the wall closing his eyes.

"What should I do Jack? I can still feel how hard she was trying to hide her pain but she failed", tear rolled down from the side of his eye.

Jack was not able to say anything as he was also not able to do anything. He was feeling bad for both of them. He just wrapped his arm around Jimmy's shaking him little to comfort him.

"Boys! Got drinks for you", Mike came inside with some cold drinks as they were working from long hours.

But coming closer he noticed Jimmy's tears he knew everything about them, he smiled, "Seems like got Cera's message finally". Jimmy smiled back and nodded.

Jack was checking what drinks he had brought.

"Hey! Where is my hot chocolate?", Jack whined like kid.

"What chocolate? Are you a kid?", Mike rolled his eyes.

"Ahhh! I told you to bring one for me", Jack was complaining like a kid.

"C'mon just drink these drinks for now", Mike said but Jack pouted.

"No, give it to this shorty!", Jack said.

Jimmy was in thoughts but he snapped back hearing Jack.

"Hey! who the hell you called shorty?", Jimmy yelled, Jack pressed his lips.

"Come here I'll tell you who's the- HEY! WHERE ARE YOU RUNNING? COME HERE!", Jimmy started to chase him making Jack laugh.

Chapter 44

At restaurants :

"Oh Hello? Miss. Cera Ford? am I talking to the air?"

Cera snapped back when the person in front of her knocked the table.

"Y-Yeah", She replied looking away. He sighed.

"I can understand your situation as I'm also going through same as you", He said and Cera looked at him surprised but he nodded.

"See, we both don't want this marriage", He said, Cera looked at him with some kind of hope in her eyes. "We need to call off the marriage".

"But how Mr. Rodger?", She asked him but shine in her eyes disappear hearing him.

"You! You can beg your dad to cancel this marriage because my father is not listening to me at all", He sighed leaning back on chair.

Cera rolled her eyes rubbing her temple.

"Will you do Miss. Cera?", He asked again hoping something.

"If only I could, I wouldn't have come to see your hopeless face here", Cera hissed madly making him gulp.

"Means t-there is no cha-"

"Shut Up! Your annoying!", She again shut him closing her eyes while thinking something.

Cera was here on a fancy forced date with her arranged fiancé. She was surrounded with her father's men, the man she was going to marry was also forced in this marriage and this thing was clear that it was not a marriage but a business deal.

Again after few days :

"Dang! What's wrong? Why isn't she sending message? It's been 4 days!", Jimmy was just looking at Jack's phone.

"She will, something might have come up. Relax", Jack assured him but here Jimmy was again being worried.

"But what? Now enough! I need to know in what situation she is! Whether she is fine or not- I….. I can't help but worry Jack", Jimmy sighed frustratedly.

"She is fine Jimmy, think positive", Jack also had no words to convince Jimmy as he himself was worried.

Being impatient Jimmy called on that number but phone was off, "I hope she is fine".

At Ford Mansion :

Cera couldn't message Jimmy because she didn't have any phone as Uncle Shawn was on leave for next few days. Cera was on verge to lose all hopes but she was holding on because she knew Jimmy was still waiting for her and he was also desperate to find a way to get her out from here.

She was not talking with anyone, not with her dad and not even with Harold. But from yesterday she was not feeling well. She was feeling so exhausted as she was not eating properly.

"Hey, here's your favourite spicy noodles with hot garlic soup", Harold came while she was lost in her thoughts. He said excitedly to cheer her and entertain her.

Cera gave him blank look and looked away.

"Hey, Cera don't be like this. I'm missing that jolly, stubborn and noisy Cera", He said but she looked at him annoyed in complete disbelief.

"Leave....", She said again looking away. He sighed.

"I'll but eat properly. I have noticed, You have been skipping meals", He said concerned.

"Why do you care? Just leave already", She was really not in mood. She had been acting like this with him.

"I do and don't make hard for yours- Cera!", Harold was talking but suddenly Cera held on table and holding her head she was trying to stand still feeling dizzy but...

"Don't need to come near me! I'm fine!", Cera said showing him hand to stop him as he was coming towards her worriedly and she stood straight rubbing her temples.

"Cera you are not-"

"I told you not to worry about me! I don't need your care! I'm not dying, I'll be fine with some painkillers! Now Leave My Head Is Aching!", Cera tried to yell but her aching head was not helping, she just wanted to kick him out.

He sighed and was about to leave but some people entered in the room with some wedding dresses, heels and other accessories for bride. Seeing all those things Cera's mind heated more breaking her patience.

"What the hell is this? who told you to bring these things here?", She yelled at them also. Harold was trying to calm her.

"Miss, Mr. Ford told us to show you these things and you have to choose from these", one of the men spoke.

Cera's jaw clenched but before she again burst on them....

"O-Ok, you may leave these here. We'll inform you", Harold interrupted and bowing little they went out of the room.

Cera glared at those things and madly stormed around and started to throw it all over the floor destroying each and everything, she destroyed all the pretty things and dresses in a snap.

"I DON'T WANT IT! I DON'T WANT IT! I DON'T WANT IT!", She shouted furiously.

"Cera stop it! Stop it!", Harold pulled her back stopping her. "Don't be silly Cera, your dad won't like it. Calm down!".

"I d-don't want these things... I-I w-want to go from h-here", She started to cry again feeling helpless.

But she started to feel dizzy again, she held her head as it was spinning and that's when she fainted and was about to collapse on the floor but Harold held her.

"Cera! C-Cera....?"

After sometime :

"It's wedding in few days now what's wrong with her? I know it's all her drama", Mr. Ford said to Harold who was waiting for doctor who was checking on Cera.

"No uncle, She has been not feeling well lately", Harold said.

"But why now?", Mr. Ford still had doubts on his daughter.

"I think, we should postpone wedding date and-", Harold got interrupted.

"NO! I have convinced Mr. Rodger for this marriage after lots of efforts. Now I will not take any risk by postponing anything", Mr. Ford again said so heartlessly which was making Harold worry more about Cera. He was feeling bad on his helplessness.

"Mr. Ford?", Doctor came out from Cera's room Harold quickly went to her.

"Yes Dr. Lia? How is Cera?", He asked worried.

"Cera is pregnant", Dr. Lia said.

There was silence for a second, Harold blinked and a small smile was about to appear on his lips but it faded hearing Mr. Ford, "We don't want that child".

Dr. Lia and Harold both looked at Mr. Ford in disbelief.

"Uncle, H-How can you say this? She is your daughter and it's her-"

"Don't dare to teach me", Mr. Ford again interrupted Harold.

Harold just gulped on his words and looked away frustratedly.

"But Mr. Ford, we need to ask Cera. Mother's consent is needed", Dr. Lia said.

"No need to ask her. I'll never let that dirty piece near me or her so you better get rid of it", Mr. Ford said being annoyed.

"I'm sorry Mr. Ford but I won't proceed without talking with Cera or taking her permission", Dr. Lia strictly said and turned to Harold, "Take care of her". And she left from there.

Dr. Lia was Cera personal doctor and like friend to her and knew everything about her health issues. But she was also well aware about Cera and her dad's relation too. That's why she was always on Cera's side but she was also not enough strong competent to go against her dad.

"Ok, Harold, find someone else and do whatever you need and get rid of that thing", Mr. Ford said and left from there. Harold looked at his back still in disbelief. He was confused if he should help Cera who was in the most delicate condition or be loyal to his boss who was the reason of his existence.

Putting her hand on her belly Cera was looking out with small smile and tears in her eyes but those rolled down when she closed her eyes.

"Jimmy.... It's our b-baby". In all these days of suffering Cera was so happy but suddenly her heart clenched realizing it was too much happiness knowing well that something really bad was coming for her.

Chapter 45

5 DAYS LATER :

Jack was feeling down as he was also worried about Cera. It's been so long that he got her message. He was going to pick Jimmy from his therapy session as they were supposed to go to studio for some recording.

He was walking and suddenly stopped looking at the sea, it was calming view and he was feeling relax. Then he realized it was the same place where he had spent some worst time of his life. He sat there on a bench.

Jack was an orphan and he grew up in an orphanage but during his high school age he left orphanage and started to live by himself. And those hard struggling days were flashing in front of his eyes when he slept empty stomach for many nights and was living on one time meal. But soon he met Cera, she helped him to find a Job and taught him how to get stable with life even when you are alone, because she knew very well how to do it. They were too young to understand life so deep with completely opposite backgrounds from each other but the suffering was same. They were alone but found that bond between them. There was not any feeling of attraction but just a feeling of pure friendship and care for each other, feeling of someone by their side.

Jack smiled through tears feeling proud on himself that he's working hard. He had found people who loved and cared for him now. He also had family. But for now, he was also feeling bad for being not able to help them in their bad.

Jack sighed and looked at his wrist watch and stood up and was about to walk but someone bumped on him from behind.

"Hey! What th-" He said but stopped when he recognized the person.

"Emma? Hi!", He smiled at the girl and helped her to pick her flowers and books.

Emma looked at him and smiled recognizing him and signed something, Jack smiled wider knowing she recognized him.

"Yes, Jack. How are you?", Jack asked.

Emma didn't say anything but was looking at him with small smile.

"Emma?", He called her and she blinked looking away, he chuckled. She again signed something……

She was mute….

Bold letters = Emma's words in sign language

"I'm sorry"

"Hehe, it's ok. How are you?", Jack again asked as he was surprised seeing her after so long.

"I'm good, how are you?"

"I'm also good. What are you doing here?", he was talking with her but she seemed little lost and flustered.

"Actually, I'm here to present my art piece in a global exhibition near Roll Hall"

Jack just blinked looking at her. "I-I'm sorry I didn't u-understand", He said pressing his lips. But she chuckled. Then she opened that poster in her hand to show him and he got it.

"Oh, You have participated in art exhibition. Wow! That's so cool", He said congratulating her.

"And what about you?"

"Umm, I got selected by SGT company and we are going to debut next year"

Her eyes widened with smile.

"Congratulations Jack"

She shook hand with him. He smiled.

"Thank You Emma".

"Now you'll be star, don't forget me"

Jack gulped again not understanding what she said and she got it, "Hehe I'm sorry". She shook her head and signed slowly to make him understand.

"Don't"

"Don't....?"

"Forget me"

"Forget me- Forget you....? Don't forget- OH you want me not to forget you...?", He blinked looking at her suddenly feeling tickles in his tummy with her smile. She looked away when he was just staring at her.

"Ok, bye. I'm late. See you again soon"

And she started to walk away.

"Huh- Hey! Wait- Emma! Your number?", He ran to catch up with her.

"At least give me your number, So w-we will be in touch, you know, right?", he was nervous to ask for her phone number.

But she smiled. She took his phone from him and dialed her number and gave it back to him. And waving at him she went from there, he was still smiling at her. He saved her number and texted her. She was on the other side of the road and he saw she checked the text message and again waved at him so did he.

He put his hand on his suddenly racing heart and sighed.

"I'll not forget you Emma".

Emma was Jack's old neighbor, she used to live next door with her father when Jack was newly shifted there. But 2 years ago Emma and her dad left that place for her dad's new business. In those days they had become good neighbors. But today meeting after so long time they both realized how much they had missed seeing each other.

Jack again checked his wrist watch and his eyes widened realizing he was also late and he ran from there.

But running little far he again bumped on someone.

"Oh NO! Owk- I'm so sorry, Are you alr- Dr. Lia....? Are you ok?", Jack apologized.

"Oh Jack, I'm good. I'm sorry I was also not looking on the way", she said collecting her stuff and Jack helped her.

"Hi, How are you Jack?", She asked.

"No, Not so fine doc", He replied with sigh.

"Hmm, because of Cera, right? Poor her, this shouldn't have happened with her", She sadly said looking down but Jack frowned.

"What? W-What happened to her?", He asked being worried.

Dr. Lia looked at him confused as Jack was Cera's friend and Lia thought he knew everything.

"D-Don't you know?", She asked concerned.

"No... What's wrong Doc? Actually, we had no contact from few days, that's why I was also worried. Did you visit her? How is she? and what h-happened to her?"

"Jack.... I met Cera yesterday and something really tragic happened to her....."

Chapter 46

"C'mon do it Jimmy. Throw it, break it, punch it or do whatever you want to do to let out that anger from you", the therapist, Dr. Hord said putting some glass things in front of Jimmy.

But Jimmy was just sitting there holding tightly on that cushion and crying silently while looking down without touching any of the things.

"Remember all those bad things people did to you, make yourself angry".

But Jimmy still didn't move because there was no anger in him, it was just feeling of regret, guilt and the pain he suffered. Doctor knew it, he just smiled at Jimmy.

"Are you ok, Jimmy?", Dr. Hord asked, Jimmy looked up and saw doctor offering him a glass of water. He took it and drank some water. Dr. Hord was one of Mike's family friends and Mike had talked about Jimmy with him and here Jimmy was being handled by Dr. Hord.

"It's ok if you don't like violence", doctor chuckled.

"Umm, do you love someone? I mean do you have girlfriend, Jimmy?"

Jimmy looked up and nodded, "Cera".

"Okey...? So you love her?"

"Yes, I love her so much".

LET ME HEAL YOU

Dr. Hord again smiled as this was the only line Jimmy spoke without stuttering.

"Do you think she does the same?"

"Yes, she loves me too".

"Now she is not with you and-"

"I miss her, I don't know how she is, what she is going through, I'm worried", And here Dr. Hord made Jimmy talk. This was the slow process but he knew Jimmy will do it.

But it was not like that for now, Jimmy was not feeling well from 2 days. He was worried and feeling so uneasy. Jimmy was missing Cera little too much for some reason. He didn't even get any message from her. He was waiting for Jack to ask him if he got any message from Cera.

"Hmm, I see and do you wan-"

"Jimmy!", They heard Jack from outside.

"It's My friend", Jimmy said and was about to go out but Jack stormed inside. Jimmy smiled thinking he got some message from Cera but his smile faded when he saw Jack's teary eyes.

"Jimmy..... C-Cera...", Jack was panting hard as he came running all the way. Jimmy's heart was racing, he was not ready for any bad news.

"D-Did you get any message from her?", Jimmy asked, Jack shook his head.

"S-She.....", Tears rolled down from Jack's eyes scaring Jimmy more, he gulped and held Jack.

"WHAT JACK? What happened to her?", Jimmy managed to ask as he was already feeling weak in knees.

"Cera w-was......p-pregnant", Jack said closing his eyes.

Jimmy became silent for a moment, he let go of Jack. A small hope entered in his heart but suddenly a whole mountain fell on him when he recalled Jack's words. He frowned in disbelief.

"W-What do you m-mean, 'She was' ?"

Jack couldn't answer.

"Jack, please t-tell me what happened to her?", Once again Jimmy was falling apart. But he decided to be strong for Cera. He got it what Jack meant to say. Jimmy knew Cera needed him. He wiped his tears.

"I want to meet Cera right now".

"Yeah, Yeah. And I know who can help us", Jack said and they left from there right away.

Dr. Hord looked at them and sipped on his coffee relaxing on his chair, "Jimmy doesn't need therapy but his Cera".

At Café :

"Please Doc, We need to meet Cera. Only you can help us", Jack said. Jack and Jimmy again came to meet Dr. Lia to ask her for help.

"Ok Jack but how?", She seemed nervous.

"Yes, I have plan", Jimmy said and they both looked at him.

At Ford Mansion :

"Dr. Lia? What brought you here again?", Harold asked.

Lia gulped before replying, "Harold, Mr. Ford has done what he wanted to but Cera is my patient and her health is my responsibility. I'm here to do her routine check-up. It's her wedding in few days she should appear healthy"

Harold nodded but saw two boys with her, they were in their doctor's attire and they were wearing mask.

"And who are these guys?", Harold asked.

"Uh- These are my assistants, they are interns", she answered confidently trying not to stutter.

???

Yes, they were Jimmy and Jack behind those masks. Harold looked at them then again at Lia and nodded, "Ok".

They three immediately started to walk but....

"Wait-"

Harold again stopped them. Lia gulped and turned to him.

"Thanks Lia"

She nodded with small smile.

"Harold, don't let anyone disturb while we are inside Cera's room. You know Cera need space. I have something to talk with her. Here is no one to care for her but I do", She said with that indirect taunt to Harold. Harold just looked down.

"Hmm".

On the other hand, Jimmy's heart was racing feeling so heavy. He was so desperate to see Cera. And then Lia signed them to move and they went to Cera's room.

As soon as they entered inside the room, they saw the whole room was messed. All things were shattered on the floor and there Cera was catching Jimmy's attention strengthless, laying on the edge of the bed. His heart clenched and tears filled in his eyes. He quickly went to her. Jack locked the door.

"Cera!", Jimmy saw she was sleeping more like unconscious. He took her on his lap. "Cera?... What h-happened? Open your eyes", He patted her cheek trying to wake her up. He removed his mask.

"Cera... it's me Jimmy. See, I'm sorry.... L-look at me. Why are y-you silent like this?", Jimmy was so worried seeing her like that. He was crying, he tried to wake her up in her way while caressing and kissing her softly all over her face.

"C-Cera... Jack, she is having fever", Jimmy looked at Jack and started to rub her cold palms.

"Doc-"

"Ok, relax let me check", Lia said, Jimmy laid Cera on bed and Lia started to check on her.

"Hmm, she is having fever and due to weakness, she fainted. Jack, give me my bag", Lia said but Jack was just looking at Cera worriedly.

"Jack?", She called him again.

"Y-yeah, she'll be fine, right?", Jack asked handing her bag.

"Yes, don't worry", Lia injected Cera and they waited for her to get conscious.

Jimmy sat near her caressing her hand.

After few minutes Cera slowly started to open her eyes but she immediately closed again feeling her heavy head, "Ahk- What the-"

But then from her blur vision she saw Jimmy looking at her worried. She blinked to get better view.

"Are you ok Cera?", He asked.

But suddenly those intense flashbacks started to play in her mind.

Flashbacks :

"Doctor, We want to abort the child", Mr. ford said.

"No..."

"NO DAD! IT'S MY BABY PLEASE!"

"DAD PLEASE....DON'T DO THIS! DAD NO! I DON'T WANT TO COME WITH YOU!"

"NO!!"

End of flashback

Chapter 47

"NO MY BABY!", Cera suddenly screamed squeezing her eyes and holding on her head.

"Cera? What happened? OPEN YOUR EYES!", Jimmy shook her holding her arms.

Cera opened her eyes and coming back to senses she again saw Jimmy and quickly got on his lap wrapping her arms and legs around him she hugged him tightly and started to cry hard. Jimmy closed his eyes preparing himself to comfort her, he caressed her back while wiping his own tears.

"Shuu....", He caressed his back.

"J-Jimmy... o-our baby.... h-he k-killed m-my baby".

Jimmy's hug tightened around her as his heart was clenching more with her every sobs.

"I-I'm sorry, I couldn't p-protect our b-baby", Cera was choking on her sobs. Jimmy was just trying to calm her but for that first he needed to calm himself. He took deep breath before facing her.

"Calm down Cera, it's not your fault. I know you tried.... It's ok, everything will be fine", Jimmy was trying hard to control his cracking voice.

"I don't w-want to be here Jimmy, p-please take me out f-from here".

"Yeah, don't-"

Knock Knock

"Dr. Lia, May I come?"

Their eyes widened hearing Harold from outside the door. But Cera was still sobbing while hugging Jimmy tight. Jimmy carried her just like that and took her inside the bathroom. Jack put on his mask and went to open the door.

Jimmy locked the bathroom's door and put Cera on the vanity. He looked at the door hearing Harold's voice understanding that he was there out in room. But when he turned to Cera his heart again dropped seeing her this much hurt for the first time, she was no more strong. She was just looking at him while crying. He cupped her face and pecked her lips and wiped her tears.

"Don't cry Cera.... You know I don't feel well seeing you like this", He placed his forehead on her. It was getting hard for him to make himself strong for her.

"J-Jimmy, my b-baby", Her head again fell on his shoulder and he broke into tears.

"I'm s-sorry, it's all my fault. I shouldn't have waited. Why d-did you stop me?", He could understand losing a part of her meant a lot to Cera and he was also feeling sad about that, it was breaking his heart but he was holding on his senses knowing for now Cera needed to move on. And he was there to help her to get her out from there.

"I know, it's hard for you. But l-let's try too m-move on Cera", he just dared to say that biting on his lips to control his shaky voice. "For us...."

He moved her back and wiped her tears stroking her hairs.

"You'll try, right?", He asked again cupping her face.

Not having any option, she just nodded slowly while still crying.

"Look at me... d-don't worry. Everything will be fine", he said and hugged her again kissing her head.

Meanwhile :

Jack opened the door, Harold came inside and saw Cera was not there.

"Where is Cera?". He asked.

"B-Bathroom.... She is inside the bathroom", Lia replied.

"Oh, sorry for disturbing but is she fine?", He asked concerned.

"No! she is not, how can you be so careless Harold? She was unconscious here and no one saw", Lia was mad.

Harold's eyes widened, "What? I did-"

"I know her father but I didn't expect this from you Harold".

Harold didn't have anything to say.

"Ahem... *cough cough*", Jack faked cough to let her know that for now she needed to send Harold out and she got it.

"Uh- y-you may wait outside, I'll show you her reports later", Lia said.

"Ok", Harold said and was about to go but he stopped again. "Where is the other guy?"

Lia gulped not finding any excuse.

"I-I sent him to bring some s-stuff from my clinic", She managed to reply something convincing and he paused but nodded.

"Oh ok", With that he left from there and Jack again locked the door.

"Jimmy", Jack called him knocking on the door.

But Cera opened the door and came out followed by Jimmy.

"Hey, are you ok?", Jack asked Cera.

She just did a small nod looking at him. She went to her bed, Jimmy poured water for her and made her drink, "Feeling better?"

"Y-Yea"

"Are we g-going from here?", Cera asked.

"Yeah", Jimmy said but...

"Jimmy, we can't. There are many guards out there, we can't take her out just like that. And what about Harold?", Jack explained as he was decided to think practical knowing Cera and Jimmy were emotional for now.

Cera looked at Jimmy. He held her hands.

"I'll take you out from here, no matter what! You trust me, right?"

"I do"

"Oh no! Mr. Ford is here, he'll be sussy about us. He is very smart", Lia said seeing him out from the window.

Cera's grip tightened on Jimmy, she looked at him with teary eyes, "Jimmy, I-I-"

"No... you are not going to cry anymore, ok? You are my strong girl! I'll come again. I need to think something to get you out from here", Jimmy kissed her hands.

"But it's wedding in two days", Jack said.

"NO! I'll not let anyone to marry you just like that, hmm? I Will Not! Before that I'll get you out from there, I promise! And now you promise me, till then you'll eat properly, take rest properly and take care of yourself. I'll try to come as soon as possible, don't worry, Hm?", He said kissing her head to assure her, she again just nodded closing her eyes.

"Look at me, say it to me. Promise me", He asked again.

"I-I promise Jimmy. I w-will wait for you".

He hugged her, "I'll come soon".

Jimmy knew it was impossible to take Cera out from there today. If anyone got even little suspicious about them then Cera's dad will be more alert and that was not good for them. To gain Mr. Ford's trust Cera needed to stay there and act normal.

"We need to leave", Jack said but Cera and Jimmy was not ready to let go of eachother.

But Jimmy moved back, "I'm Sorry, Just 2 more days".

He kissed her forehead again and wiped her tears. He got up putting on his mask.

"Now Rest and take medicines on time", He covered her.

Jack came to Cera, "Take care. And this, keep this". He handed her a cell phone.

"No, now I'll only talk to you, when we'll meet again. I don't need this", Cera said looking at both of them. Jack nodded.

With that they were about to go out but Jimmy looked at Cera for the last before going out and Lia noticed.

"Don't worry Jimmy, I'll again come to check on her. And I'll stay with her until you came back", Lia smiled to assure Jimmy.

"Thank you, Dr. Lia".

Chapter 48

Wedding day:

"Miss, will you please stop crying? I'm not able to put on eye liner. We need to finish your make up on time", The make-up artist said to Cera.

Cera looked away again wiping her tears, "I'm sorry".

Cera was waiting for Jimmy. But somewhere she was nervous and scared too. She couldn't help and more tears started to fall from her eyes.

"Is my princess ready?", Mr. Ford came inside. Cera's expressions turned blank. Everyone went out leaving them alone. He looked at Cera through mirror.

"Oh My My! Look at you, You are looking so pretty. Cera, you have grown up so fast honey. I still remember holding your small hands for support when you were stepping for your first walk. Now I'll hold your hand while walking through aisle and I sti-", he was talking while wiping his fake tears but Cera interrupted...

"I wish I shouldn't have held you for any support ever", She said sending him cold stares.

"I'm your dad Cera, Why are you talking with me like this?", He asked playing innocent and she scoffed.

"Dad? Dad is superhero for his daughter and you are being the super villain of my life", She chuckled sadly.

His fake innocent expressions turned cold again.

"Aren't you bei-"

"Are you done? You are annoying!", Cera said rolling her eyes.

"It's useless talking to you! Get ready fast, I'll come again", Mr. Ford was controlling his anger for today and stormed out from there, leaving Cera again in tears.

"I know you are coming Jimmy, but please make it up fast. I can't hold in here anymore". Cera was all alone in the room, only her low sobs could be heard but then……

"Cera?"

Cera heard a whisper call. She stopped crying and looked around but there was no one. She was about to shrug but again...

"Cera?"

Her eyes slightly widened she stood up looking around finding the source of the voice. She was alert.

"Cera, Help me"

She again heard and followed the voice and walked towards window which was slightly opened. She peeped and saw someone was there, her eyes widened seeing a guy in a suit was literally swinging on the window.

"What the heck! Are you crazy? It's fucking 6th floor! Who the hell are you?", She yelled being shocked. "Do you wanna di-"

"Hey! Will you please stop yelling? I'm here to help you. First help me!", He said trying to pull himself up.

Cera gave him her hand for support and managed to pull him inside the room. He leaned on the wall while catching his breath. Now Cera was little nervous as she had helped a weird stranger not knowing if he was really there to help her or not.

"W-Who are you?", Cera asked.

He didn't say anything and went to lock the door.

"Hey Hey! What a-are you doing?", She again asked but he again went to another side where there was another window, he opened the window wide. He looked at you and smiled and signed her to come there. She gulped and slowly went to him and looked out of window, she gasped covering her mouth with her hand seeing that heart-warming surprise and tears again filled in her eyes.

"Jimmy...."

Jimmy was there on a huge crane ladder with flowers. He was wearing a black tuxedo with set hairs, he was looking groom and giving all prince's vibes. He smiled with that shine in his eyes as soon as he saw his Cera, he was not able to take his eyes off her. But he snapped back when tears fell from her eyes.

"Are you gonna stay like that forever?", that unknown guy said extending his hand to Jimmy for support and pulled him inside and closed the window.

"Hey! I'm out, open the window!"

He heard Jack from outside, he bit on his tongue for forgetting Jack was also there.

"Oops- Sorry", He again opened the window and helped Jack also to get in.

Meanwhile, Cera hugged Jimmy, "You came...."

"So were you waiting", He said pulling her closer.

Cera moved back from hug and was about to kiss Jimmy but.....

"No Cera, your Lipstick!", That unknown guy said.

"Oh yeah, right", She said and just placed a peck on Jimmy's cheek leaving a pretty lip mark.

"By the way, who are you?", Cera asked him.

"I'm Joy, Jimmy's friend", He said with bright smile.

Cera also smiled and looked at Jimmy, "Friend".

"Now enough, Let's go from here before anyone catch us", Jack said glancing at the door.

Cera and Jimmy nodded looking at eachother.

"Wait, are these for me?", Cera asked pointing at flowers in Jimmy's hand.

"Nope, It's for your dad. In exchange of his flower like daughter as I'm stealing her today", Jimmy said making her slightly blush which she was trying to hide with laugh.

Jack scoffed as he found his friend cheesy, "Seriously? Not tha-"

"Aww! They are so cute", Joy was adoring them meanwhile and Jack gave him weird look.

But suddenly they heard knock on the door followed by , "Miss. Cera..? Are you ready? Bride maids and waiting outside".

They all looked at eachother with wide eyes.

"Miss. Cera?", the man from outside of the door again called her. As he was not getting any reply he again knocked on the door.

"Miss. Cera open the door or else I need to-"

Suddenly Jack went to door and slightly opened peeping out.

"What? She is getting ready, Give her time, okey? It's her wedding", Jack said with holding on door.

"Mr. Pros, what are you doing here? You are not allowed to meet her", that man said trying to peep inside but couldn't catch any sight.

"Why? I'm her best friend and she invited me, any problem?", Jack replied.

"No but I need to inform someone", He said and left from there.

"Yeah yeah, go and inform whoever you want, I'm not scared of anyone and I don't care!", Jack said again closing the door and sighed in relief pressing his back on the door.

"We don't have time, we need to make it quick", Jack said again coming to them.

"Yeah, Cera, let's go!", Jimmy said holding her hand and she nodded, but when she went to the window, the ladder was missing. They had removed ladder because it will take time to step down from the ladder. Cera looked at Jimmy confused.

"Yeah, we are going to jump from here", Jimmy said noticing her questioning expressions. Her eyes widened.

Chapter 49

"W-What?"

"Don't worry, ther-" Before Jimmy completes Cera hugged him tightly wrapping her arms around his neck.

"Hold me tight and Jump", Cera said hiding her face in his neck. Jimmy smiled realizing how much she trusted him.

"Hey, relax. Nothing will happen, see there", Jimmy said caressing her back and pointed down from the window. She slowly moved back and saw there was Mike and one other guy with him with some huge stunt bags holding for them.

But before they move the door flung opened as Jack had not locked it.

And there was surprised Harold, "Jimmy? Jack...?"

Cera gulped nervously looking at Jimmy, Jimmy held her firm to assure her. Everyone was looking at Harold.

"Hey Harold, Plea-", Jack couldn't complete when Harold said, "What are you looking for? Just Jump already!"

Harold closed the door and locked it.

"Go! I have been handling securities and cctv from long, now I can't do it anymore just leave before they come here", Harold said surprising them.

"Y-Yeah", Jimmy and Cera again held eachother and were about to jump……

"Cera......", Harold called her, she turned to look at him, He paused, "I'm sorry for everything.....Take care".

He waved at her but she didn't say anything and Jimmy jumped out of the window along with her.

Jack went to Harold and hugged him, "Thank you".

"Yeah, and give this to Cera and Jimmy as their wedding gift from me", Harold said giving Jack an envelope. Jack saw what it was and smiled.

"Take care of her, Now Go!", Harold again said patting his back. And with that Jack and Joy also Jumped off the window.

Meanwhile :

"AAAHHHHHHHHHHHHHHHHHHH!!!!"

Jimmy and Cera were falling down from the window and....

THUD

They fell on that stunt bag safely.

"AAHAHHHHHHHHHHHHH!!!!"

"Hey! Why are you screaming now? You are safe", Mike said.

Cera opened her eyes finding herself safe. She was on the top of Jimmy while he was still holding her protectively. They both were looking at eachother breathing heavily.

"I Love You"

"I Love You Too!", Jimmy said placing a tight-long kiss on Cera's cheek making her giggle.

"So, Are you planning your honeymoon also there?", that unknown guy with Mike asked.

"HELL NO! not here", Cera made weird face looking at him.

Jimmy carefully got down and helped Cera to get down.

"Now, who are you?", Cera asked that guy.

"Hi, I'm Rain", he introduced smiling at her.

"Oh, one more friend. I'm Cera".

LET ME HEAL YOU

"I know", He said, Cera smiled at Jimmy.

"Ok I'll get the car", Mike said going from there.

"Actually, we are-"

"AAAHHHHHHHHHHHHHHHHH!"

Jack and Joy were screaming too while falling down.

THUD

"Why do you guys have to scream while falling?", Rain asked rolling his eyes.

"Yeah, Jump from there, then you will know", Joy said catching his breath.

"HEY!"

They all turned to the voice and saw some security guards. The manager and other Mr. Ford's men were coming towards them.

"Run!", Jack said and they all started to run from there. Seemed like Harold failed to handle cctvs and guards. They started to chase them.

Cera was running once again carrying her huge and heavy wedding dress.

But while they were running....

"Cera! Stop Right There!"

Cera slower her speed and stopped so did Jimmy.

"YOU ARE NOT DOING IT RIGHT! YOU KNOW THE CONSEQUENCES!"

Mr. Ford was yelling as he was far from them. Everyone stopped as Cera did, she was panting with mixed feelings. She looked at Jimmy who was looking at her and turned to her father.

"DO YOU THINK I CARE NOW?"

She again held on Jimmy's wrist with one hand and other was holding her wedding dress and......

"Jimmy, RUN!!"

Jimmy's eyes widened as she suddenly pulled him along with her. He was just looking at her while running, it was going on in slow motion for him. Her hair strands were waving with passing air, those slow blinks of her eyes, she was glancing behind while running with slight panic expressions as they were chasing them again but Jimmy was like hypnotized by her.

And he smiled......

"Cera.....?"

"WHAT?"

"You are looking so beautiful..." He said literally while running out of breath.

"Huh-", She laughed out loudly looking at him not knowing what got into him suddenly.

"Thank you, Now run silly!", She said while still laughing. He smiled and held her hand.

His friends were already waiting there with car, they made up to there and quickly getting into car they left from there, leaving those guards and Mr. Ford behind.

After sometime :

"Are they still following us?", Rain asked while driving.

"No I guess, they are following Jack's Car", Jimmy said while glancing behind.

"Hmm, switching cars was the best idea", Rain said with wink.

"Umm, it's really nice to meet you all but who are you guys?", Cera asked still not having clear identity about those new two faces.

"My friends", Jimmy smiled so she smiled back knowing he really found some good friend circle.

Chapter 50
FLASHBACK :

A *Day before wedding day :*
"Yes, one more time she will be running from her marriage but she'll be definitely getting married tomorrow", Jimmy had that bright smile. Jack also smiled looking at his friend so confident, Jimmy noticed it.

"W-What?"

"You are different", Jack said.

"What do you mean?", Jimmy asked with slight frown making Jack chuckle.

"You look more confident and....COOL", Jack ruffled his hairs.

Jimmy pressed his lips while looking down, "Because I want her, I can't lose her. NEVER!"

"Guys, Our group is completed now! we got 2 new members", Mike said coming in and 2 new faces also entered with him.

They just shared smile.

"So shall we start with introducing ourselves?", Mike asked.

"Yeah sure. I'm Rainend Jeff, you can call me Rain. I can sing as well as rap and I'm the lead guitarist of our team", One of the new boy said introducing himself.

"Hello, I'm Crison Joy but you can call me Joy. I'm singer and song writer. And also a drummer for our team", And the other one introduced himself.

"Ok, I'm Jack Pros, you can call me J-Pros. I'm Lead vocalist of our team".

"Hi, I'm Jimmy Tolger and you can call me......"

Everyone was looking at him.

"Jimmy......", Jimmy said and they chuckled. Jimmy had not decided his stage name yet but he was comfortable to go with his original name.

"I'm song writer, Sub-Vocalist and Lead dancer for our team", Jimmy ended his introduction with slight bow.

"And I'm Mike Carter, also known as-"

"MICKEY-C! THE LEADER OF THE GROUP!", They all said in one go. Mike chuckled scratching back of his neck.

"Yes and I'm the lead rapper and the producer for our team, Nice to have you all in team guys!", Mike said and they all celebrated.

They were eating and drinking together to get along and then Jack got notification on his phone. He looked at Jimmy and took him little away from them.

"What?", Jimmy asked.

"This is the venue", Jack said showing his phone to Jimmy.

"Hmm..."

"Now what are we gonna do?", Jack asked as Jimmy seemed to be thinking. Jimmy put his hand on Jack's shoulder.

"We have many things to do buddy, but we need more people", Jimmy said looking at rest of the boys. Jack raised his eyebrow, Jimmy smirked.

"Guys!", Jimmy called them and walked towards them.

"Will you help me w-with something?", Jimmy asked.

But they just smiled looking at eachother.

"We know what help you want", Joy said. Jimmy blinked looking at them confused.

Rain walked to Jimmy and put his hand on his shoulder, "Mike told us everything. We'll help you, it's gonna be our first team work".

Jimmy smiled and with Rain's words he felt so connected with them and assured too.

"We are glad to be part of your love story", Mike smiled at Jimmy.

"Thank you", Jimmy smiled looking at them all.

End of Flashback (Present Time):

"Thank you so much", Cera said.

"Yeah, thank you all for helping us", Jimmy was really grateful to finally get these friends.

"Still, it's not over until your wedding", Joy said.

"Yeah, lemme call Jack to bring Mom at venue", Jimmy said confusing Cera.

"Where? Where are we going?", And she asked.

"Huh- don't you know?", Rain looked at Jimmy confused asking him if he had told her or not yet.

"Why do you think we are wearing these suits and all ready for?", Joy asked already questioning Cera.

She looked at Jimmy and saw he was blushing.

"What?", She again asked.

"You are getting married with Jimmy today", Rain said.

"WHAT?", She frowned, they got startled.

"W-Why? What happ-"

"STOP THE CAR!"

Chapter 51

"Stop The Car!", Cera cut Jimmy and asked to stop the car.

"Wait- Why? They might be coming, it's no-", Rain tried to explain but……

"STOP.THE.CAR!!", She again commanded pressing every word.

Rain pulled the breaks and Cera immediately got off the car making Jimmy nervous he also got out behind her.

"Cera? Cera, what's wrong?", Jimmy asked nervously.

"Did you ask me for marriage?", She asked confusing him.

"What? Now? First, we need to leave from here Cera", He said trying to convince her.

"No, I'm not going to marry you until you ask me", She said and Jimmy sighed.

"Ok fine. Cera, will you marry me?", He asked as she said.

But she replied with "NO!"

"Why? Now what?", Jimmy was worried about getting caught again but here Cera was not as if she was ever.

"Not Like this! not for just a formality! I want proper proposal or else I'm not gonna marry you! BYE!", She said turning around and started to walk away from him while madly holding her huge wedding dress.

Jimmy didn't know what to do as he knew how stubborn Cera was.

"Cera! Cera wait- Listen Cera!", He followed her but she didn't spare a glance to him.

But then she stopped hearing him....

"Don't go leaving me this desperate my love, please come back".

"I love you and I want to do it for rest of my life. My heart belongs to you, my soul belongs to you Cera. I want you in my life", He said and saw her turning around.

She turned around smiling and saw him on his knees. He smiled and continued, "I know you are always with me but I want to make you officially mine. I want to give name to our beautiful relation".

"You have become that precious part of me, without you my life has no meaning, without you I have no meaning. And yeah I have not planned anything so I'll just ask....."

Cera's eyes started to glitter with tears, her heart was beating so fast even though she knew what he was about to ask.

"Cera, would you like to spend rest of your life with me? I promise to keep you always happy and cherish our love....."

"Cera, Will you marry me?"

Cera was so lost in him that she snapped back when her tears fell. He was smiling at her and of course he had ring too, He pulled out small box from his pocket revealing a beautiful ring with shining stone but not more that her eyes. She was shedding happy tears capturing him, that view in her eyes, clicking her memories. She wiped her tears and ran towards him.

She stopped in front of him and chuckled seeing the ring as she had not expected that. He was looking at her waiting for her answer.

"Yes, I will"

She said controlling on her cracking voice.

And they heard claps as their friends were cheering from the car while looking at them. He smiled even brightly. He gently held her hand and was about to slip the ring but she pulled her hand back and thought something.

"What are you thinking now? Look Cera, don't scare me on every point like this please", he said with pleading eyes made her chuckle again.

"Nothing, I-I just want to change. I don't want this dress", She said with small pout.

"Why? We are going to marry and you are perfect, pretty enough....... to take my breath. Why do you wanna change?" He said and stood up.

Cera was trying hard not to blush as Jimmy was flirting out of his range today.

"Because they forced me to wear this dress for someone else. I don't want it, I want to get ready for you, I want to look pretty for you. I want to be your bride", She said playing with his bow tie with little pout.

Jimmy paused blinking at her but smiled finding her cute and pulled her in a hug. He was amazed like what kind of girl she was.

"Why are you so cute? Ok, as you say", Jimmy pecked her head. She smiled hugging him back.

"And this ring, wear me in our wedding ceremony", She said

"Ok, now let's get you new dress", He said but she moved back and seemed hesitant.

"I'm sorry, new dress woul-"

He cut her by pecking her lips, she pressed her lips and he laughed catching her blushing again.

Jimmy had understood her hesitation about buying a new dress would be expensive and she didn't know if he had money as she had demanded without thinking anything about it. She was looking down, he cupped her face and made her to look at him.

LET ME HEAL YOU

"Don't worry hon- Now I'm able to give you what you deserve. For me nothing is expensive and precious than you", He said slowly stroking her hairs.

Cera couldn't help but blush more and quickly hugged him hiding it from him but he noticed and laughed. He picked her and went to car.

Jimmy and Cera again got into car and his friends again clapped for them. Cera smiled and hugged Jimmy's arm and they again drove from there.

"Joy, call Jack and ask where they are or if those men still behind them", Rain said.

"Yeah, I texted Mike. He said they are not being followed anymore, they are going to pick Jimmy's Mom", Joy replied.

Jack and Mike were in another car. They did it to trick their followers.

"I knew it, they will not follow for long. Now Mr. Ford must be consoling 'my couldn't be husband's father and all his rich relatives", Cera said sadly scoffing. "Now he'll ask for new deals and he will even try to look for me tomorrow if he gets to convince them successfully, and if he fails to convince them then, he won't bother himself to see my face ever again....... I don't care anyways".

Jimmy felt sad for her, wrapping his arm around her shoulder he pulled her close. She smiled.

"And how do you know?", Joy asked.

"Do you think this is my first time running from my wedding?", She said and there was silence for few seconds.

"Oh.... G-Good", Joy gulped smiling nervously.

Chapter 52

There were not much people but Jimmy's Mom, his friends and Mike's Mom. They all were waiting for the bride. Jimmy's eyes were checking on entrance with every passing second. And then.......

Suddenly everything became in slow-motion. Those wild butterflies in his stomach were briming tears in the corner of his eyes. His Cera was coming to him slowly, Mike was bringing her to her groom. Holding flowers in her hands, she was walking while lowering her eyes. Jimmy was watching her, so elegantly and beautifully walking into his life.

That new gown was less expensive than the previous one but was looking prettier than that expensive one. And of course Jimmy's heart was not in mood to calm down as it was jumping in his chest threatening to come out.

Cera slowly lifted her eyelids and looked at Jimmy and smiled, and there he forgot how to breath.

"Hey Tolger! Are you inviting bugs to enter your mouth? Close your mouth dude!", Rain said and Jimmy immediately pressed his lips together making everyone laugh.

Mike gave Cera's hand in Jimmy's and he held it gently. Jimmy started to breath deep but slowly and when she was near him, he whispered, "Stop doing this Cera, My heart can't handle this much. It's going crazy I Swear!".

She chuckled, "Calm down Mr. Tolger, there are many things ahead". His eyes slightly widened but he calmed himself down.

They both stood in front of eachother, holding hands, looking into eachother's eyes with so much love and affection. And they started to repeat the vows after priest getting all the flashbacks from their love life, that shared pain, sorrow and comfort and preparing themselves for better.

"In the name of God......

"I, Jimmy Tolger take Y/n to be my wife, to have and to hold from this day forward, for better, for worse, for richer, for poorer, in sickness and in health, to love and to cherish, until we are parted by death"

"I, Y/n Take Jimmy Tolger to be my husband, to have and to hold from this day forward, for better, for worse, for richer, for poorer, in sickness and in health, to love and to cherish, until we are parted by death"

"I announce you as husband and wife, you may kiss the bride"

As priest announced Jimmy cupped Cera's face and wiped her tears.

"I Love You", He leaned and pressed his lips on her. Cera closed her eyes, finally her dream came true.

She held on his arm when he pulled her closer deepening the kiss. Everyone started to cheer for them, their people were so happy for them.

"Ahem.... You may continue at home, right?", Rain said and they all laughed.

"I Love You Too", Cera said moving back but again hugged him. But Jimmy notice something was off with Cera suddenly. Her mood was suddenly down, she didn't have that smile anymore but the fake one looking at everyone. He moved her away to take look on her and asked raising his eyebrows "what's wrong?", but she just shook her head while smiling, she hugged his arm. But Jimmy still doubted her smile.

Cera was looking at everyone, those happy faces made her genuinely smile. Then she saw Ella, in no time she went to her and hugged her tightly and started to suddenly making everyone silent. All were looking at her, only her sobs could be heard in that hall. Ella carssed her back to comfort her.

"Ayii! What's wrong with my baby? It's a happy moment, don't cry dear", Ella said kissing her head. She probably knew the reason why Cera was crying.

"You should move on honey; everything will be fine. Don't think much, you are the strongest I ever know. I'm always there for you", Ella said and moved her back cupping her face.

"I know, you are looking the prettiest today", She wiped her tears and kissed her cheek.

Cera went back to Jimmy. Jack came to them.

"Umm, this Harold gave me this to give you guys as your wedding gift", Jack said handing Jimmy an envelope.

"What is it?", Jimmy took it from him and opened it and read it, "4 days-3 nights newly wedde- ahem..... c-couple h-honeymoon package", He looked at Cera and laughed awkwardly.

"We don't want it", Cera replied coldly without even looking at it.

"Yeah act-"

"He prepared for you both. He'll feel bad", Jack said cutting Jimmy in mid-sentence. Jack knew Cera was mad on Harold but Jack didn't want her to break any relation with Harold.

"I don't care, I don't want anything from him. And Jimmy doesn't have any time, also has his schedule, you should know that", Cera said still being cold.

Jack sighed and he knew how stubborn Cera was. And Jimmy also didn't want it as it seemed expensive, He wanted to take Cera on some trip but by his own.

"Yeah, it's ok if she doesn't want. We'll go but not any soon but whenever she wants", Jimmy said to assure Cera.

"Fine! C'mon now don't give me that look", Jack said pulling her in a hug. She smiled little and hugged him back. Jack moved away from her and jumped on Jimmy, Jimmy caught him and hugged him back. Jack held their hands and said, "Congratulation to both of you, stay happy and you both deserve eachother. Always stay by eachother no matter what. I Love You Both". He was about to kiss on Jimmy's cheek but Cera pushed him away so he kissed on Cera's cheek. They all laughed.

Cera and Jimmy met everyone they clicked pictures together for their beautiful memories, laughing and giggling.

While everyone was busy taking pictures, then Jack saw someone on the entrance which made him smile.

"Emma...?"

He went to her all smiling, she smiled. She did small wave at him.

"Am I late?", she asked in her sign language.

"No, please come", Jack welcomed her.

Cera elbowed Jimmy to show him Jack was with a new girl. Jimmy saw and raised his eyebrow, she chuckled. They saw Jack was bringing her towards them.

Emma smiled at Cera and gave her flowers which she had brought for her. She turned to Jimmy and did a slight greeting bow Jimmy smiled back and did the same.

And Emma said something in her sign language which was obvious that she wanted to congratulate them. Cera looked at Jimmy and then at Jack.

"I'm mute", Emma said in her sign language. Cera didn't want to pity on her but her eyes softened.

"Thank you so much for coming", Cera said holding her hands.

"This is Emma my friend and my old neighbor", Jack introduced.

"Oh, Nice to meet you, Emma. Thank you for coming", Jimmy said properly greeting her.

"You guys look so good together".

Cera and Jimmy smiled at eachother. Emma's signs were simple to let them understand what she was saying.

"Jack always talks about you guys, he told me about your love story"

Umm, it wasn't that simple though. Cera and Jimmy looked at Jack.

"She's saying, I talk a lot about you guys", Jack said looking at Emma and Emma nodded making him smile.

"I really wanted to meet you guys"

"She wanted to meet you guys", Jack again explained her.

"Aww! That's so sweet of you", Cera said and hugged her.

"Please enjoy the feast", Jimmy said and she nodded. After taking some pictures Jack took Emma to introduce to others. Cera and Jimmy smiled looking at eachother. They were observing Jack and his smile while looking at Emma.

"Is she...?", Jimmy asked doubtfully. Cera sighed, "I guess so". They chuckled.

After a small feast, they all were ready to go home.

"Umm, Jimmy, Today I'll go with Mrs. Carter. We ladies are going to have sleepover tonight", Ella said.

"Yeah, so both of you can have your night- uh- I mean have your time", Mrs. Carter said and they chuckled. Cera pressed her lips looking down while Jimmy was already blushing mess.

"Ok m-mom", Jimmy simply replied.

Chapter 53

"Everyone is well experienced so they decided not to waste time on training period. And tomorrow we are going to record our first song. I'm so excited and nervous too", Jimmy was talking while laying on bed and hugging Cera. He was telling her about boys and some new things he experienced after he had joined the company.

"All boys are so co-operating, helping and lovely. I feel like I know them from so long that I don-", Jimmy stopped talking when he noticed Cera was not listening to him but was lost in her own thoughts while gripping on his shirt.

"Cera...."

She didn't answer. "Cera....?", He again called her gently stroking her hairs but she flinched with gasp making him worried. She sat up.

"I'm s-sorry, I d-didn't hear you", She said being flustered. She was sweating.

"It's ok, calm down. What were you thinking?", He asked caressing her back. She didn't say anything, He got off the bed to get water for her. He made her drink some water.

"Hey, aren't you feeling well?", He asked while touching her forehead to check if she was having fever or was sick.

She calmed little down but suddenly her tears fell and she quickly wiped it.

LET ME HEAL YOU

"What happened Cera? Are you tired? You should rest", He said again making her to lay on bed but she sat up again and hugged him.

"Jimmy, I'm scared of being happy", Cera said and Jimmy remember her saying this something like this before also.

"I'm r-really happy t-today and it scares me the most. I can't be happy for so long. Few days ago we were all happy together but got separated. T-That day when d-doctor told me that I was h-having....a baby, I-I was so happy Jimmy, I wanted to tell you that, I had thought everything would be fine now but that happiness also c-couldn't stay any long.... I-I lost my b-baby Jimmy....and now ......"

Jimmy pulled her closer, he could understand that many bad things happened one by one which Cera was not able to get over. It was traumatic but still she stood strong and was trying to move on and what he could do was to only comfort her.

"Don't think like that Cera. Think positive, think about us. Nothing will happen", He said caressing and kissing her head to comfort her like an ideal husband.

"Are you hungry? Wanna bite on something? I'll make it for you", He asked thinking some food might lift up your mood.

He was about to get up from bed but she stopped him holding his wrist.

"Yes, I wanna bite on you", She said pulling him closer and slightly bite on his cheek then down on jaw and continued to his neck. She looked up to see his closed eyes, she caressed his cheek, he opened his eyes and smiled.

He was about to go for his turn now but she stopped him, "Opps- Sorry..... Not now Mr. Tolger , I need to take shower first".

She moved him little away and stood up ready to go towards bathroom. But at the very next move she was pushed and pinned on the bathroom's door with sudden flip by her dear husband. She saw his naughty smirk and gulped nervously.

"J-Jimmy....I-I-"

"Why are you so nervous?", he leaned closer to her face, "I also just want to take shower".

He brushed his nose with hers giving her goosebumps and he was playing with her hairs and giving her light tickles.

"O-Ok, Y-You can go first", She said trying to act strong under his sudden dominance.

But he chuckled on the way she was nervous as few minutes ago she was trying to be bold. She closed her eyes feeling his hot breaths on her lips.

"No.... I want to shower with you.... Lemme help you to wash up today", he said and suddenly opened the door of bathroom. She was about to fall back but she didn't even flinch as she knew he was going to hold her.

"Let's shower together Baby", He said and she snapped back.

Her eyes widened and she stood straight, "What?"

"Yes!", He said and pushed her inside the bathroom and he also went in.

"AYYY!! JIMMY TOLGER! You Pervert!", She yelled.

"Whatever you say my love because I'm your husband now", He replied calmy removing his shirt and turned the shower on.

Cera gasped as she was still wearing her wedding gown but they again laughed. Jimmy pulled her by her waist and kissed her under the shower, she closed her eyes kissing him back.

After Two Years

Chapter 54

He was so pretty on that huge screen. His eyes were shining while looking around the crowd, like he was looking at his new life.

His smile.....

That's what all Cera wanted in her life. In this last two year Jimmy got all the success and fame he deserved. His hardwork paid off so well. Leaving all his fears, anxiety and all insecurities behind he made it. And Cera always supported him and never left his side. She always looked at him being a proud wife to always let him know that she was always there and he was doing great. Cera was cheering him from the crowd, she loved seeing him on the big screen.

It was Jimmy and his band *'Shooting Stars'* very first concert which was fully crowded. In very less time they had become pretty popular among youngsters. Their music and unique style were attracting audience.

They were done with their performance and was talking with their fans, telling them how they were feeling right now. And it was Jimmy's turn and the whole crowd went crazy when Jimmy took the Mic.

"Damn- he is so hot", Cera said to herself but then she heard some girls fangirling over Jimmy.

"Hey Tolger! Why Are you so fucking Hot?!", A girl shouted pissing Cera.

"Hey! Watch your language, he is my husband", Cera said loudly.

"Oh really? Mine too", That girl mocked and laughed not knowing who Cera really was.

Well, that wasn't Cera's first time, she just shrugged and focused on Jimmy.

Jimmy looked at crowd in awe, he was surprised. He was not able to speak and he chuckled.

"Thank you so much", He humbly bowed to his fans.

He continued, "Thank you so much for everything you guys have given to us. I always read your letters which sometimes make me so emotional knowing how much you all love me. We all will always be thankful to our fans for liking our music and us. I really was not able to make it alone, our group members who always supported eachother and pulled ourselves over here and for me this meant alot."

Crowd cheered loudly. Jimmy again continued, "And today-"

And here Cera's Baby husband broke into tears not able to talk making all crowd go "Awww".

"Ayyiii! Our baby Jimmy is crying", Mike said wrapping his arm around Jimmy's shoulder.

"Heyy! Don't cry my bro", Jack said from behind.

"Aww....our baby need hugs", Rain said hugging Jimmy from behind. They all were teasing Jimmy. Everyone laughed making Jimmy smile.

"Yeah, I won't cry. I'm just so happy today, I also wanna say something", Jimmy said making the crowd silent, "Here is someone who was always by my side whenever I needed, today whoever I'm only because of that person. Who always encouraged me, always made me realize who I'm, how strong I'm, taught me how to fight with hard times, gave me all deserving love and care when I needed it the most".

"That person is my wife....."

"WOAHHHH!", the crowd cheered loudly when Jimmy mentioned about his wife.

"She is here, I know she is not up there in the balcony but somewhere here in the crowd looking at me", He said trying to find his Cera in the crowd.

"And I just want to tell her that...... I Love You Wifey!", He shouted followed by crowd shouting......

"We Love You Jimmy!"

And on the other hand Cera's heart was racing, melting with his every word. Feeling lots of emotions with huge smile on her face she was looking at him on that big screen, She also screamed back, "I LOVE YOU JIMMY!"

Time Skipped After Concert :

After concert Jimmy straight went to his manger.

"Miss. Sarah, where is Cera?", Jimmy asked as soon as he entered in green room.

Sarah sighed already knowing he'll ask this question first. She lifted those coats from the couch and revealed Cera sleeping while cuddling Jimmy's jacket. Jimmy smiled.

"She came from backstage and told me to wake her up when you come, so should I wake her?", Sarah asked.

"No No, let her sleep. I'll take her", Jimmy said covering Cera again.

"Ok but other boys are ready to leave so?", Sarah asked again.

"Umm no, today I'll go home with Cera. But don't worry I'll be there for tomorrow's shoot", He said. Sarah nodded and left from there. Jimmy had shifted to his company with other group members because it was easy for him to catch up with his schedule but he also missed his home, his Cera, His Mom there. But now it's gonna be rest as concerts had just ended and so he wanted to spend some time with his wife.

Jimmy looked at Cera who was sleeping all unbothered about her surroundings. He sat beside her while staring at her with that loving gaze as always feeling so much peace, like he was charging himself after a long tiring day. He chuckled when she scrunched her nose in a sleep. He slowly wrapped her in his coat like a burrito and carried her to take her home.

At home :

Jimmy brought Cera home. It was their new home which Jimmy had bought 4 months ago. He was trying his best to give his family what they deserve.

Jimmy carried Cera inside the bedroom and placed her on bed. Cera was not completely asleep as she was aware of what he was doing. He laid beside her and pouted, he started to play with her lips, nose and hairs, trying to wake her up but also didn't want to disturb her sleep, so he was trying to wake her 'accidently'. He knew that she was not really sleeping so deeply. He pecked her lips and she chuckled.

"What are you doing?", She laughed opening her eyes.

"Why are you sleeping?", Jimmy asked with sad pout.

"I'm Tired Jimmy, I screamed a lot today for you guys, my throat hurts", She said turning to other side. He chuckled and hugged her from behind.

"But Honey, I missed you", He said and started to snuggle in her neck giving her tickles. She giggled.

"By the way, you guys just rocked. I really had fun", She said again turning to him. He smiled.

"Did you hear what I said?", He asked about his confession infront of all his fans.

Her smile grew and she nodded rapidly, "One more special moment is added to my memories".

"But what are you doing here? Jack told me that you guys were going to have some party after concert", Cera asked caressing his hairs. He melted to her touch and kissed her hand.

And suddenly hovered her, "Because I also wanted to have some special, beautiful moments with you".

Cera blinked as he was looking straight into her eyes letting her to see his love, passion and what's coming next. It's been 2 months that they both were away from eachother, and they both had missed eachother so much.

Jimmy leaned in and Cera closed her eyes to feel his aggression on her lips but instead she felt a soft kiss on her forehead and then on nose and then on her lips. She opened her eyes and saw him smiling.

"Good night Honey", He said and hugged her.

Cera blinked once more as he just rested his head on her chest and hugged her. She mentally slapped her forehead on her silly thoughts and smiled and closed her eyes again hugging his head and caressing his soft locks.

Chapter 55

"Doctor, How is she? She has woken up, right? Whe-"

"Mr. Rocky, Please calm down. She has just woken up, you can't meet her immediately. We need to do her check ups and monitor her mental state. Please give us some time", Doctor said to Rocky who was desperately waiting to meet her but Rocky just nodded.

"And Who is Jim-….Jimmy? She is calling his name", Doctor said, Rocky paused and looked at her from blinds.

"Jimmy Tolger……", Rocky said.

"Is he that new boy band's Member…?", Doctor chuckled.

"Yeah", But Rocky replied seriously while thinking something.

After meeting Jimmy and Jack that Rocky never tried to face Jimmy or meet him again because he knew if he does so it would bother Jimmy more.

But then Rocky saw her moving again they entered inside.

"Hey… Lexi", Rocky held her hand. Doctor started her check her.

"J-Jimmy…..", She slowly opened her eyes and saw that blur figure near her. She blinked weakly to clear her vision.

"No Lexi, it's me….. Rocky", He was so scared for something bad like her memory lose.

"R-Rocky"

"Yes….Rocky", He tried to keep her awake. She looked around.

"Hmm, patient is having no mental disorder but still she needs to recognize and accept new things. She needs time to sped up her brain. She needs well rest. She will be fine in few weeks", Doctor said smiling at her.

"Thank you doctor", Rocky shook hand with doctor, he was beyond the happiness seeing his love back to life.

After Few days:

"9 years....?"

Tears rolled down from her eyes.

"Don't cry Lexi, we lived all those together. I have captured each and every moment for you", Rocky said kissing her hand. He quickly wiped his tears when he saw she was looking at him.

"And what got into you? Why are you crying? You were not like this back then. You have changed", She asked and there he couldn't control his tears anymore.

"I missed you....", that's what he could say while controlling on his breaking voice.

Tears were falling from her eyes also looking at him, realizing so many things and regretting so many things. She cupped his face and kissed him.

"Thank you Rocky, for not leaving me alone, for loving me this much", She said and hugged him tight.

Again After A week :

"Oh No! You have broken my ear already Cera! You sing horrible, Stop it!", Jimmy yelled trying to stop his forced to be singer wife from messing his beautiful lyrics.

Cera slapped on his shoulder. Everyone was laughing on husband-wife's bickering. Jimmy was singing and recording his new solo song in their studio while Cera was trying to match his high notes making it funny.

LET ME HEAL YOU

"Look Cera, How to hit it-", Mike said trying to teach Cera Jimmy's high notes but being rapper he was also as horrible as Cera in singing.

"MaKe Me fEeL For YoUuUuUuuuuuuuu!!", Mike sang and Cera copied him and others closed their ears as the high note was out of control and everything was in so chaos.

They again laughed.

"Hehe....No I guess, I should try some other day", Cera said being unsure about her singing and Jimmy sighed.

Cera had become good friends with other boys also. They always found Cera cute and they liked to See Cera and Jimmy going lovey-dovey and sometimes bickering. Whenever they feel low they called Cera to boost up their mood. She always encouraged them for the best.

While they were laughing and talking a call boy came, "Jimmy sir, someone is here to meet you".

Jimmy looked at other boys confused, "Umm, but we can't meet fans here in studio, isn't Miss. Sarah there?"

"Yes, she is there, but that person really want to meet you urgent. He is not listening. He is actually requesting so much", boy was telling Jimmy, confusing him more.

Now Jimmy looked at Cera but she also seemed confuse.

"Ok, ask them to wait in waiting hall, I'm coming", Jimmy said and he left from there.

After sometime when Jimmy went to see the person and saw a man backing him, "Excuse me sir?"

And the unknown man turned around with a small smile. Jimmy's breath like stopped for fraction of second but he managed to silently gasp.

"H-Hi...", he was hesitant but Jimmy was numb. It took few seconds for Jimmy to reply.

Jimmy was feeling same anxiety which he had forgotten from last one year. His ears started to get warm but he didn't let go of his control over himself and tried to breath normally because some flashbacks were already started to play in his mind.

"Hi R-Rocky...", Jimmy managed to reply.

"Nice to see you again Jimmy, You guys are rocking everywhere....I'm....I'm big fan of yours", Rocky started casually.

Jimmy brought up a force smile, "T-Thanks".

"Can we sit and talk?", Rocky asked.

.

.

.

"Why?"

.

.

.

Jimmy looked away, "Actually I-I hav-"

"Isn't your wife with you? I wanna meet her too, Someone is here with me to meet you both. Will you please call your wife also?", Rocky asked. Jimmy was confused, He really wanted to go from there but still he was curious.

Jimmy told one boy call Cera.

"Sit.....?", Rocky asked and unwillingly Jimmy sat there looking down.

"I'm sorry for suddenly appearing like this", Rocky spoke again.

Jimmy looked up at him, "I-It's ok".

"And I'm sorry.... For everything Jimmy".

Jimmy paused looking at him but looked down playing with his fingers.

"I know it means nothing to you but trust me I was scared to face you again. I wanted to apologize but I didn't dare to meet you again. Yeah, I was really unfair to you. I was blinded with hate for you, I-I", Rocky didn't know how to explain himself and show how guilty he was.

Jimmy was not saying anything.

"I Know, I don't deserve to be forgiven but please try to forgive me. It's hard to be under this heavy guilt", Rocky lowered his head while joining his hands infront of Jimmy.

"I-It's Ok", That's what Jimmy could say at this moment. He had many things going on in his mind, He wanted to speak many things but words were not coming out of his mouth.

"And You know-"

Cera interrupted Rocky by entering in. She suddenly slowed down looking at Rocky and then at Jimmy.

"Oh.... Hello", Rocky greeted.

Cera gave him forced cold smile and went to sit with Jimmy. She could read Jimmy's eyes like how desperate he was to run away from there. She held his hand giving slight squeeze and he felt that relief of someone being from his side which he always felt by Cera's presence.

"Nice to see you both again", Rocky said to break the awkward silence.

"I'm sorry Mrs. Tolger, I'm really guilty for whatever happened back in past, You had to go through a lot because of me. I'm here today, to clear all the things, I hope you will listen to me", Rocky tried to sound as polite as he could. Rocky started to tell the whole past story and misunderstanding from his point of view. Cera was sitting there coldly, understanding somewhere but she was still not convinced to forgive Rocky for his unacceptable behavior towards her and Jimmy all these years.

But on the other hand Jimmy was still fidgeting with his thoughts, he was not understanding or listening to Rocky as it was hurting him more. Rocky's presence and those memories were still literally possessing him.

"Rocky, I can understand. But we have moved on with our lives and really don't want to recall those things. I don't know why you are here but we still need time. It's deep and takes time to heal properly and your presence bothers my husband. So I request you to avoid this sudden visits", Cera was cold but also tried not to sound rude.

"Oh ok, I'm sorry", Rocky looked down but he got call from someone on his phone. He smiled while talking on phone and hung up. He turned to Cera and Jimmy with the same smile.

"Will you please wait for few minutes? I'll be back.... Didn't I tell you someone is her to Meet you? I need to bring her, So just....", Rocky said while going towards elevator.

"What? Wait- ok-", Cera said but he had already gone. She looked at Jimmy.

"Relax Jimmy".

And he nodded.

"Hey, What's wrong? Who is there? And why-", Jack came there while asking but Cera signed him to shut up for now so he gulped.

Chapter 56

After few minutes Rocky came back with someone.

"Jimmy....".

That familiar voice made Jimmy to look up, His heart shook seeing the person. He got up, Cera looked at Jimmy confused and then at that unknown girl. He was looking at her. She smiled and started to walk towards him.

"L-Lexi....", Jimmy said making Cera's eyes wide, She looked at Jack who was as shocked as her.

Jimmy felt that flip in his stomach, he had seen Lexi after so many years, he had almost forgotten how she looked. And yes she was different but still he recognized her getting again those sudden attack of horrible memories. His hands were trembling, He didn't want to remember those things now but his mind was out of his control, he also wanted to meet Lexi but something in him was pulling him back. His eyes lowered and were filled with tears when she came and stood infront of him. He was scared for some reason.

"Jimmy", She raised her hand to touch him but he flinched and moved a step back, his tears fell.

Cera was still holding his hand. He was still looking down. Lexi could see how disturbed he was, she gulped down her nervousness and put her hand on his cheek.

She chuckled, "You have changed a lot, Looking so cool, huh? Just like a rockstar".

Jimmy was still feeling uncomfortable with her touch as he was blinking continuously like she was going to hurt him. He didn't mean to act so but the thing was happening to him was taking over him and he was helpless.

Lexi wiped her tears, "I saw your MVs and saw you on TV. Your concert, You have lots of fans and all, that's what you had dreamt of, right? I'm Happy that you made it buddy", She was talking while controlling her breaking voice.

"Aren't you gonna say something? Aren't you gonna talk with me Jimmy?", She held on his shoulder.

"Look at me Jimmy, I know you are mad on me.... I'm sorry buddy", She hugged him and started to cry.

And that's it.....

Those harsh words and noises started to eco in his head.

"Rocky.... Jimmy was forcing on me...."

"How cheap you went Jimmy! How can you do this to your friend just for the fucking money?"

"GUYS THIS LOOSER IS HERE, HE SHOULD BE PUNISHED WELL! HOW SHAMELESS HE IS TO SHOW UP IN SCHOOL AFTER DOING ALL BAD THINGS TO HIS OWN FRIEND!"

"SHAME ON YOU JIMMY TOLGER! Such a fake friend you are!"

"You are Monster! Devil behind that innocent face of yours!"

"He is rapist! He is a Psycho! He used his own friends and killed them!"

"MOM!!"

"M-Mom....", Jimmy mumbled and Cera felt his hold loosening on her hand. She looked at him and saw him closing his eyes.

"Jimmy? What's wro- Jimmy!"

He was about to fall on the floor being unconscious but Cera and Lexi both held him.

"J-Jimmy? What happened to him?", Lexi started to pat him to wake him up.

"Jimmy? Wait- I need to take him from here", Jack said and immediately carried Jimmy. Cera was about to follow him....

Lexi Stopped her, "What happened to him?", she asked worriedly.

"Lexi... uh- I know you- We have many things to talk, I'll tell you some other day please. I need to go, excuse me!", Cera couldn't say much as she was worried for Jimmy and she left behind Jack.

After sometime at Home :

Jimmy slowly opened his eyes and saw ceiling of his bedroom. He rolled his eyes to little side and saw Cera was sitting near him all worried.

"Hey, Are you feeling better?", She asked brushing her fingers through his hairs. He didn't say anything and just stared at her. He sighed and shifted his head on her lap and held her hand. She caressed his head.

"Are you ok?", She again asked. He nodded kissing her hand. But then he heard.....

On TV :

"And he suddenly fainted during rehearsal in their studio according to our sources, fans are worried for their beloved singer. People have crowded near the-"

channel changed

"Well known artist and member of popular group 'Shooting Stars' Jimmy Tolger got sick during rehearsals and fainted in the recording studio. But doctors said no need to worry, he is fine and co-"

TV Turned off

"What doctor? Which Doctor? We didn't even take him to doctor. This media thing is really pissing me off. They know nothing about the true incident and show things making by themselves", Ella said who was listening to news about her son on TV. Jimmy chuckled on how mad she was on media.

"Jimmy? Oh you are up", Hearing him Ella slowly walked towards bed and sat on bed searching for Jimmy, Jimmy held her hand and shifted his head on her lap curling himself like a baby.

"It's ok mom, Don't be mad", He said putting her hand on his cheek.

"NO it's not ok, why are they calling my fit and fine baby sick?", Ella said being annoyed again.

"Haha, yea, I'm fine mom".

"Ok, I'll make soup for you", Cera said ruffling his hairs and smiled, she got up and Jimmy blew a smooch to her. She went out.

Ella kept caressing him. "Were you scared to meet her?", She asked out of blue. Jimmy sighed, "I guess".

"I'm sorry Jimmy, I couldn't protect you back then my son", She said kissing his head.

He just looked at her with small smile, "I love you mom".

In their lives everything was fine and everyone was happy, just one thing Jimmy felt bad for was he was not able to give his mom her eye sight back. They asked many doctors but they said it's dangerous for her to undergo any surgery of her eyes. That thing always made Jimmy sad that this new technology and his money also couldn't help his mom. But the relief was, she was happy and proud mom.

Jimmy suddenly hugged his mom.

"Aww, my baby", She hugged him back.

"Don't watch news or medias for few days", She said and he laughed.

"As you say mom", He said kissing on her cheek.

Chapter 57

She was sitting and waiting at the bus stop. She saw all buses were leaving one by one and people were also leaving. It was already evening. She sighed looking around and looked at her wrist watch. Dark clouds covered the setting sun indicating it was going to rain any soon. She checked her phone and again sighed. She called him but the number she was trying to call was out of coverage area.

"Where is he?", she thought to herself.

And the rain started to pour. She gasped and tried be under that small roof of bus stop. She looked around worriedly as she didn't even had umbrella and no one was there to help her. It was getting late and the person she was waiting for was not showing up. Before it's too late she needed to reach home.

She took deep breath and was about to step in a rain but she saw someone was coming towards her. A man wearing all black, due to rain and darkness she couldn't see him properly, he was even wearing mask covering his head with cap of his hoodie. She gulped nervously when he was walking straight towards her. He was near, she held on her bag tightly and stepped in rain and was about to walk away but that man held her hand catching her off guard and scaring her, she pushed him away and started to hit him non stop with her bag.

"Hey! Hey! Emma! Emma!! It's me! Jack!!", He revealed himself infront of her before she breaks his neck.

She stopped panting hard but sighed in relief when she saw him. But she again started to hit him.

"Aishh, Hey stop-", Jack held her hand.

"You Scared me idiot", she said in her sign language.

Jack laughed nervously, "Hehe, I'm sorry".

"Why are you wearing clothes like this? Are you going to rob bank?"

He laughed but stopped immediately when he saw she was annoyed.

In this two years Jack had learned her language and also he had become expert in reading her eyes so it was easy for him to understand what she was saying.

"Ahem.... No, you know I can't go out just like that now a days. My fans surround me wherever I go. And it's hard to get away from them. So I covered myself like this to avoid any crowd", He said scratching back of his neck.

"Then why did you come? You should have just texted me-"

"I missed you", He said and she paused looking at him. Her eyes softened and she looked away to hide her smile.

"Hey, I'm sorry, you had to wait in rain", He said holding her hand. She smiled making him smile, "Let's go somewhere".

"Like this....?, She signed at herself. They both were all drenched.

"Umhmm.... Let's go?", He said and just dragged her in rain. She smiled while running in rain with him but suddenly she stopped. He turned around and looked at her confused.

"What?", He asked and covered her with his jacket. But she held his hand and started to dance. He chuckled and danced along, they both were dancing in rain.

One of the most beautiful and romantic thing to do with your partner, isn't it? She was dancing and he was just staring at her with that eyes full of fond and love.

Jack was in love with Emma from very long but didn't dare to confess as he didn't know what she felt for him. He didn't want to ruin their friendship either. Sometimes he felt that hint of love from her but she was never clear about her feelings, she might be insecure about something and just wanted to be friends with him, that's what he guessed. She had told him not to forget her after becoming superstar but she didn't know that she had become part of his emotions and his habit which he didn't want to miss ever.

Jack snapped back when he felt that splash of water on his face, he saw her laughing. He smiled unconsciously stepping close to her. She stopped dancing looking at him, his smile was making her heart go wild as always. She gulped when he tugged her wet hairs behind her ear and gently held her jaw. she saw his gaze landed on her lips, her breaths became heavy when he gently held her hand caressing it. And her heart exploded when she saw him leaning to her lips, unconsciously she also closed her eyes and felt his wet and warm lips on her which she couldn't resist and kissed him back. Getting her permission his hand sneaked behind her waist and he pulled her close, her fists curled on his shoulder but suddenly she pushed him away snapping him back. He quickly stepped back being all flustered.

"I-I'm sorry E-Emma..... I'm s-so sorry....I-I", Jack was too flustered to even look at her. He suddenly turned to leave but again remembered she was alone. He was just looking around but not at her who was just looking at him worried. She slowly held his hand to calm him down and he looked at her. And her eyes were enough to calm him down. He gulped and looked at their hands. Rain stopped.

"M-My car is t-there....", He said pointing at his car and she nodded slowly. They walked toward his car.

Jack turned on the A\C and gave Emma towel to dry herself and her hairs. He was drying himself, keeping his head low while taking secret glances on her but she caught him. They both just sat there in his car without saying anything.

"I'm sorry", Jack said and saw her doing the same sign.

"I didn't mean to push you like that"

Jack frowned slightly understanding what she meant.

"I didn't want anyone to see us...."

"K-Kissing"

Jack paused looking at her while processing if he was getting it right what she was trying to say or he was misunderstanding something.

"Y-You didn't- It means you wanted-..... Ahem..... You.... M-Me-", Jack smiled understanding it when she looked away while blushing. They both were looking out of window while blushing. Jack pressed his lips to control his smile. They both turned to eachother at the same time and laughed.

She looked down, he held her hand and she again looked up into his eyes and he spoke, "I Love You..... Emma".

She smiled, he saw that nervousness in her eyes.

"Do you love me?", He asked.

She gulped fidgeting with her thoughts but looking into his genuine she slowly nodded.

"I love you so much Jack"

She said in her cute sign language. But Jack saw her glittering eyes with some kind of fear or nervousness. She was confused or not sure about her feelings which was confusing Jack.

"Hey, what happened? Are you ok?", He asked cupping her face.

"I trust you Jack", She put her finger on his chest.

"I can't speak, you won't leave me aft-"

"Marry me!", He said and saw colors of her face changing.

"Will you marry me Emma?", He asked suddenly making her calming heart to race again. She looked at him blank to know if he was really serious and yes he was.

He held her both hands. "Do I ever need your words to understand what you want to say? Your eyes speaks more Emma and I love to read them. I can do this for rest of my life without getting tired. For that you just need to trust me , I'll never break your heart".

"I trust you Jack! I do Jack!"

She said and her tears fell. He quickly wiped her tears and cupped her face clicking her forehead with his.

"I'm Sorry.... I didn't mean to doubt your love, I just-"

"I Know... I know, you just didn't want to get hurt", He caressed to calm her down as she was crying already.

"Now say it will you-"

And before he completes, she again pulled him in a kiss, he smiled and pulled her on his lap kissing her back. She moved back smiling in tears and....

"I'll marry you"

His smile widened and he started to kiss her all over her face, she giggled and he stopped. He opened the drawer and pulled out a small fancy box and opened it, her jaw dropped looking at the ring. He laughed on her expressions.

"I always keep it with me", He said surprising her more. He wore her ring and she hugged him tight and now she kissed him all over his face. They both laughed and hugged.

"I Love You....", He said.

She smiled and kissed his cheek.

Chapter 58
Few days later :

"Jimmy", Cera whined coming into bedroom while Jimmy was talking on phone. He signed her to wait for a second, she pouted and sat on the bed.

"Yes Miss. Sarah, I'll talk with Mr. Bill don't worry", Jimmy saw Cera was sulking. "Wait a minute Miss. Sarah", He excused Sarah and turned to Cera.

"What is it Cera?", He asked.

"Talk to your Sarah!", She said and turned away just to let him know that she was really mad. Jimmy sighed.

"Cera, If it's not that important, Can we talk later? Please?", He requested and again talked on phone. Cera looked at him in disbelief and stomped out from the room.

"No I'll do that and also I'll send you some recording, Jack is also here at my place today so we can record together", Jimmy went busy in talking on phone.

After he was done, he turned around, "Now tell me, What do you want?"

"Huh? What do I want?", Ella asked.

Jimmy saw Cera was not there but his mother was coming in, "Oh, Cera was here".

"Ok, umm will you ask Mike to drop Mrs. Carter at our home, it's been long we have not met", Ella said.

"OK Mom, I'll call Mike. By the way have Jack left?", Jimmy asked.

"No, he is on video-"

"YAH! Tolger! Are you done clinging on your wife? How much do I need to beg you for one game?", Jack came inside yelling. He wanted to play video games. But Jimmy was not in mood as he had got their new schedule.

"Jack, Miss. Sarah had called me and asked me to record the first verse of Rain's Lyrics", Jimmy said.

"What? But why so sudden? I'm not prepared", Jack whined.

"Oh c'mon, you are always more than prepare Mr. Pros. Just get your fine voice", Jimmy said to hype Jack.

"Hehe, I'm not that good", Jack said ruffling his hairs and agreed to record.

"So, I think you need Mike also here, I guess", Ella said.

"Right Mom, I'll ask him to come for stay with his mom and-", Jimmy stopped speaking when they heard some noise from kitchen.

"Cera...."

They all went out to check. As soon as they entered kitchen Jimmy's eyes widened seeing Cera was unconscious on the floor. He rushed to her and held her.

"Cera? Cera....? Hey.... Wake up?", Jimmy patted her but she didn't show any movements. He quickly carried her out from kitchen.

Jimmy gently laid Cera on the couch.

"What's going on? What happened?", Ella asked being worried and stumbled on steps.

"Careful Mom. Relax, Cera is unconscious", Jack said holding her hand and brought her near Cera.

"What? Cera...", Ella sat near Cera while rubbing Cera's palms.

Jimmy sprinkled some water on Cera's face, he was worried too. Cera flinched and fluttered her eyes slowly opening them.

"Cera... C'mon, wake up. Are you alright?", Jimmy asked worriedly brushing her hairs. He helped her to sit up and sat beside her.

"What's wrong honey? Aren't you feeling well?", Ella asked checking Cera's forehead.

"Nothing Mom, I-I'm fine....", Cera said even though her head was heavy and she was still feeling dizzy.

"Aren't you eating well? Why did you faint?", Jimmy asked caressing your head. She didn't say anything.

"Drink some water", Jimmy said bringing glass to her lips.

"No, I don't want to.....", Cera said holding his hand.

"Have some, you'll feel better", Jimmy still asked her to drink.

"No Jimmy... I don't...", She again said and moved his hand away but he still insisted and made her to drink water and here she lost it....

"I SAID NO JIMMY! I DON'T WANT TO DRINK THAT FUCKING WATER!! YOU GOT IT?", Cera yelled hitting the glass away.

Her sudden outburst startled them all. Jimmy gulped and got away from her and stood beside Jack being shocked and scared of his wife.

"Okey....but why are like this? I just gave you water", Jimmy said in tiny.

Cera suddenly started to cry. Ella sighed and pulled Cera in a hug.

"Ok ok, calm down", Ella caressed her. Perhaps she knew what's wrong with Cera.

"Mom, Tell them not to annoy me", Cera said while crying.

"Huh- what do you mean by them? What did I do? I didn't even ask you to drink water", Jack said not wanting to be Cera's pray.

"Why? WERE NOT YOU PLAYING VIDEO GAMES HERE WHILE SCREAMING WEIRDLY? I even told you not to make noises, I REALLY WANTED TO THROW THAT PAN ON YOUR FACE", Cera again yelled while crying.

Jack gulped and moved behind Jimmy. "Bro, what's wrong with your wife today?", Jack whispered to Jimmy who was also puzzled.

"Shuu! calm down Cera. And you two, stop bothering her", Ella said moving Cera away and wiped her tears.

"What is it? Are you feeling something?", Ella asked cupping Cera's face.

"Y-Yae", Cera said wiping her nose.

"Are you sure?", Ella asked again.

"Yes Mom", Cera said and Ella smiled and kissed her forehead.

Both boys were so confused with ladies' conversation.

"I'm so happy, are you happy?", Ella asked.

"Yes mom, I'm so happy", Cera said while crying and again hugged her

"Aww, it's ok. It happens. Calm down baby", Ella kept caressing Cera until she calmed down.

Jimmy and Jack were still looking at eachother all confused.

"Ahem, Will anyone explain us also? If it's not bothering Cera....", Jimmy said very carefully.

Cera moved back and shot a look at Jimmy.

"I-It's ok, We don't want to know", Jimmy said pulling Jack from there but Ella laughed.

"But you need to know Jimmy", Ella said and Jimmy stopped.

"Come here Jimmy", Ella said and Jimmy came to her and knelt infront of her.

And she suddenly smacked his head.

"Ouch! Mom?", Jimmy rubbed his head.

"How come you didn't realize such thing about your wife? Idiot!", She said confusing Jimmy more.

"W-What have I d-done?", Jimmy asked nervously feeling so dumb. He looked at Cera and then again at his mom.

"You are going to be father dumbo!", Ella said giving Jimmy those mixed emotions. It took few seconds for him to recall what his mom just said. He paused looking at Cera and blinked but when he realized his eyes widened and a huge smile of surprise grew on his face.

"Wha- R-Really?", He held Cera's hands while looking at her with those stary eyes but she was still giving him that mad look.

He laughed, "AYheyyyy! CERRAAAA!!!".

But suddenly that guy from behind picked Jimmy up, "Yeayyyyy!! WOAHHHOOOOOOOO! JIMMY TOLGER!! YOU MADE IT BRO!! YEAHYYYY!", Jack shouted spinning Jimmy around.

"Hey! What The Fuck! Put me DOWN!", Jimmy yelled, Jack put him down and hugged him tightly.

"I'm GONNA BE UNCLE!!", Jack let go of Jimmy but he was still shouting. Cera covered her ears as it was too much for her. Her head was aching with noise.

"I'm going to tell Emma!", Jack said and ran from there.

Cera's eyes widened but before she could stop him he had left. Tears fell from her eyes, it was nothing but her mood swings and because of symptoms. Jimmy was just staring at Cera with same loving gaze, he was too overwhelmed to speak. He again sat beside Cera.

"Mom, you are going to be grandma", Jimy said, he was too happy. He didn't know how to express his happiness. Ella chuckled.

"I know, now I'll leave you two alone and you better take care of your wife", Ella said and got up to leave.

"Yes Mom! I Will!", Jimmy said and Ella left from there.

"Mom, but I didn't-", Cera said but Ella had gone. Cera wanted Ella to stay with her. Jimmy was looking at Cera as she was still crying silently.

Jimmy sighed and pulled Cera on his lap and she immediately hugged him, now he was understanding what was wrong with her.

"What happed to my Baby? Calm down sweetheart... I'm here, tell me what you want", Jimmy caressed her whispering sweet things to calm her down.

"Don't t-talk to me.... Everything is irritating me. My h-head is aching. I wanted to eat pasta that you always make for me and you just ignored me", She was still crying, Jimmy felt bad.

"I'm so sorry Love, I'll make pasta for you. I'll do everything you say, don't cry please", He said again as sweetly as possible.

Chapter 59

After sometime Cera was calm and eating her pasta while Jimmy was smiling at her.

"Why didn't you tell me?", Jimmy asked and she looked up.

"I-I also got to know this morning, I was planning to tell you after eating pasta but you were busy talking with your Sarah", She said while stuffing her mouth with food.

"Hehe, I was just talking about work. Ok I'm sorry", He said wiping sauce on her mouth with tissue.

"Cera, I promise, I'll always protect our baby and you", Jimmy said and Cera felt those butterflies whenever he talked something like this.

"Are you happy?", She asked. He smiled holding her hand.

"Is this even a question? I'm beyond the happiness. I'm like, I'm having that weird mixed feeling, I'm excited and also bit nervous. But I'm ready with lots of love for both of my babies", He said slightly pinching her stuffed cheeks. Cera smiled.

"Hushh! Finally got that smile', He said dramatically wiping that non existing sweat from his forehead.

Cera chuckled and continued eating.

"How's it?", He asked and she simply fed him. "Umm, I'm genius!", He praised himself and she agreed. And he again stared at her.

"Jimmy"

"Yes?"

"Don't you feel like, I'll give more attention to baby than you?", Cera asked.

"Huh? No, Why would I? It's our baby and we should give in to love and nourish it, right?", He gave very logical answer.

"But I'm feeling like you'll give more attention to our baby than me", She pouted and Jimmy laughed.

"Oh, so here's your point", He said still laughing on her cuteness.

She was done eating and got up and started to walk away. Jimmy followed her and picked her up.

"Hey.... You both are same to me. As I said earlier, I'll love both of my babies equally", He said walking towards their bedroom while carrying her. She giggled and hugged him but soon he put her on bed and was about to move away but she stopped him. He looked at her confused.

"I'm craving again", She said.

"And what is it? Just tell me, I'll make anything for you", He asked being surprised.

"You", She said and before he could react, she pulled him on bed and kissed him roughly.

He smiled and laid there letting her to do what she wanted. She slightly bit on his lips, he wrapped his arms around her and switched their positions and kissed her.

"Baby, Our baby is watching us", he said between the kiss.

"So what? let it know how much mommy-daddy love eachother", Cera said pulling him closer. They both chuckled.

After few weeks :

Jack was nervous and Jimmy and Cera were comforting him.

"Just sing a song for him", Cera suggested.

"I want to marry his daughter not him", Jack said giving her 'Are you serious?' look.

"Don't be so nervous Jack, just be yourself", Jimmy said while adjusting Jack's collar to hype Jack's confidence.

Jimmy and Cera had arranged a family dinner and invited Emma and her Dad so Jack would tell about him and Emma to her father and also talk about the marriage but Jack was being so nervous for no reason according to Jimmy but Cera was fueling Jack's nervousness.

"Hey, handle if I mess anything", Jack said to Jimmy.

"You'll do great don't worry", Jimmy said but he looked at Cera just to see her pressing her smile. He signed Cera to say something.

"Y-Yeah, You'll do great! You are a pop-star Jack!", Cera said patting Jack's back but Jack looked at her being more worried.

"Emma's Dad doesn't like pop music", Jack said nervously.

"Ahem... Uh- I don't know", Cera ran from there leaving him with Jimmy.

"It's ok, Calm down, Take breath. He is just your girlfriend's Dad", Jimmy said but it seemed like not working much.

"Jimmy! They are here", They both heard Cera from outside, Jack's eyes widened but Jimmy pushed him out and went along.

Jack tried to pull on smile, Emma did small wave at him.

"Hey Jack! How are you? Long time no see", Emma'S Dad greeted Jack.

"Yes Uncle, Nice to see you again", Jack also greeted him back sharing a small hug.

"Hello sir, I'm Jimmy Tolger", Jimmy introduced himself.

"Woah! Who doesn't know you guys! Very nice to meet you! I'm Jaeson Luis, Emma's Dad", Emma's dad introduced himself.

"Nice to meet you too sir, this is my wife Cera and my Mom", Jimmy introduced his family.

"Hello Mr. Luis", Ella said.

"Hello uncle", Cera greeted. Emma came to Cera.

"Hey how are you?", Cera asked and they both started to talk.

After sometime they all started dinner while talking and laughing but Jack was still not able to talk to Mr. Luis. Emma and Jimmy were encouraging him secretly to talk.

"Ahem.... Thank you for having us for dinner", Mr. Luis said and he noticed some whispers.

"Jack, Do you have anything to say?", Mr. Luis again asked, perhaps he knew it already but still he wanted Jack to ask.

"Uh- .... I-I- Yeah.....", Jack stuttered and looked at Jimmy but he looked away.

"Yes?", Mr. Luis said focusing on him.

Then Jack eyed on Cera, Emma and Ella and then again Looked at Mr. Luis.

"Uncle, I.....I Love Emma....", Jack said finally and continued as Mr. Luis was listening calmly, "We Love each other and with your permission I want to marry Emma".

Mr. Luis looked at Emma and then again at Jack, there was a silence for few seconds. Cera and Jimm looked at eachother worried as Mr. Luis seemed serious. Emma was also nervous.

Mr. Luis chuckled making them all to look at him, "You took too long to say it. As Emma had told me about you, I thought you would be so excited for marriage but look at you, why are you so nervous?", Mr. Luis teased Jack. They all laughed.

"Oh Boy, Thank you so much for coming in my Emma's life. She always talks about you. She has changed a lot since the day she met you again, she has become cheerful, happy and so confident about herself. She has that fond of you Jack, she has already told me about you guys. I came here just to meet you", Mr. Luis said making Jack's face to light up. He smiled at Emma.

"Of course I'm giving permission".

"Yeahyyy", Cera cheered and started to clap so they all did.

"Thank you, Uncle", Jack said.

"I trust you boy, take care of my daughter from now on, she is yours", Mr. Luis said emotionally but Jack nodded genuinely to assure him.

"Congrats Jack", Ella said finding him.

"Thanks Mom", Jack said and went to hug her.

Chapter 60
After Five Months :

Jimmy looked at Cera and smiled, she hugged his arm and they both looked at their friend getting married.

Jack kissed Emma and everyone cheered for them. It was secret marriage just in the presence of close friends and family to avoid media. But Jack had already told his fans that he's getting married but when, it was a secret.

Jack moved away from kiss and looked at Emma and hugged her, "Here you are mine". She chuckled kissing his cheek.

Everyone started to congratulate them and take pictures. Cera and Jimmy also went to them.

"Congratulations Bro!", Jimmy hugged Jack.

"Thank you bro!", Jack hugged him tightly.

Jimmy tried to move away but Jack was not leaving him. Suddenly they became silent when they heard Jack sniffles. Jimmy smiled little and carssed his back to calm him down.

Emma was looking at Jack, she knew he was overwhelmed. Cera came to Emma and hugged her, "Congratulations Emma".

Emma smiled Looking at Cera and saw her small baby bump, **"How are you? And How's baby?"**

Cera didn't understand what she was saying but she got it that Emma was asking about baby, "It's 25th week, baby is fine and I'm also good".

Jack moved away from hug and turned to Cera and hugged her.

"Ayyy, Congratulations buddy", Cera said patting his back.

Jack moved back and held their hands and was looking down as he was not able to stop his tears.

"Thank you for being my family".

Cera touched his cheek and wiped his tears.

"Hey, Stop crying, Emma is watching", Jimmy said cleaning Jack's face and fixed his hairs and then pushed Jack near Emma, they all laughed.

Emma held Jack's hand and they smiled at eachother and it got caught in a camera.

After sometime everyone was eating, dancing and having fun and Cera was smiling while looking around and her husband was as always looking at her. She caught him staring at her.

"Control your stares Mr.Tolger, I'm already yours", Cera said and chuckled.

"I want to merry you again, Why are you so pretty?", Jimmy flirted holding her hand and put on his chest. She laughed which made him smile.

"Come sit here", He took her to sit as she was standing from long.

"Are you ok? Do you wanna go home?", He said giving her water.

"No, I'm fine. I want to stay here", Cera said so he sat beside her.

"Did you eat well?", He again asked caressing her baby-bump.

"Yes I ate but I want to eat ice cream again", Cera said with puppy eyes.

"No! not ice cream. You have had enough of ice cream, It's not good Cera", Jimmy said and Cera looked away folding her hands.

"Hey, I have something else to show you", He said and she looked at him. He smiled.

"What?", Cera asked excitedly.

"Let's go", He said holding her hand.

"Huh? Where?", She asked but he took her somewhere.

Jimmy took Cera out from there and Cera saw Sarah was already waiting for them.

"Hi Cera", Sarah greeted Cera.

"Hi Sarah, How are you?", Cera asked.

"I'm Good Cera, how are you? And what's up with baby?", Sarah asked, they started causally.

"I'm fine, baby is also doing well. But Are we going somewhere?", Cera asked, Sarah looked at Jimmy and Jimmy nodded. Sarah came behind Cera and blind folded her.

"What? What are you doing?", Cera was confused.

"Relax, I'm here. Just come with me, there is a surprise for you", Jimmy said holding around her shoulders to keep her near.

"Surprise?", Cera asked again excitedly.

"Yes, come here. Careful", Jimmy slowly guided her.

Cera was smiling all along but Jimmy stopped so she did.

"Are we here?", Cera asked, Jimmy chuckled on her excitement.

"Ok, we are here. Open your eyes slowly, ok?", He said slowly removing Cera's blindfolds.

Cera blinked to clear vision and saw a familiar black sports car infront of her, her eyes widened realizing something. She looked at Jimmy, he smiled.

"T-Toyo....?", Cera said and went near and again realized....

"N-No, it's not Toyo", She looked at him while touching the car.

"Umm, no it's not Toyo but, It's look a like", He said making her chuckle.

"For you", Jimmy went to her, "Do you like it?"

She looked at him with loving eyes and hugged him. She was not only happy for the surprised but she was emotional, feeling so blessed and lucky to have him. The thing was he kept note of her every small thing which made her happy. She had that emotional connection with her car but he had made her to forget about it but he himself still remembered. She kissed on his cheek and moved away smiling.

"I Like it, thank you so much. But this car, you didn't have to spend so-

"I Love You", He said staring at her with smile and her tears fell. She didn't mean to cry but she couldn't control her tears.

"I Love You Too", She said and again hugged him. He gently picked her. She chuckled, he took her to door and opened it for her. She got in, and he also got in from other side.

Cera put on seatbelt and was ready for first drive, she looked at Jimmy but he was just looking at steering while holding it.

"What? Let's go", She said excitedly.

"Uh- y-yeah. Actu-"

"Yes, start the car. Where are we going?", She asked again but he looked at her nervously.

"Cera, I-I don't know h-how to drive", He said, Cera looked at him like dumb but laughed.

He looked down.

"Hehe, it's ok. I'll drive", She said getting off the car.

"No Cera, how can y-you?"

"Come out", Cera said opening door from his side.

"But-"

"Umhmm, Com out', She pulled him out.

Cera got the steering and Jimmy on a passenger seat.

Cera started the car and drove off.

"S-Slow, Are you ok?", He asked.

"I'm fine Jimmy, where are we moving to?", She asked.

"Wherever you want!", He said and she smiled.

"Woohooo!", She goofed opening the roof of the car, Jimmy smiled and got up closing his eyes.

"It feels so good..... WOAHHHHOOOOO!", He said spreading his arms.

Cera looked at him and smiled, she wanted to see him like this, having his time with that satisfaction and relief on his face.

After sometime they came into city and then Jimmy's eyes caught some street dancers were dancing on the same place where he used to dance.

"Cera, stop...."

"Huh- What?", She stopped the car and looked at him and saw where he was looking and she also realized. She smiled, Jimmy looked at her and again at those boys. Without thinking anything Jimmy got out of car. Cera's eyes widened as she knew crowd will go wild if they see Jimmy.

"Jimmy wait-"

But then, some bodyguards surrounded him. Jimmy was also surprised but saw Sarah who was just behind them all the way with those bodyguards in their company's car.

"Hey! Isn't he Jimmy Tolger from Shooting Stars"

"Yes, It's Him! OH MY GODDDD!!!"

"He is Jimmy Tolger!!"

"See Jimmy Tolger!"

People started to come near Jimmy taking pictures and making videos but Jimmy was still looking at those dancing boys but they also stopped seeing the unexpected crowd and saw Jimmy.

"Hey It's Jimmy!", One of the boy said and they all went to see Jimmy not knowing Jimmy himself was coming to see them.

Jimmy was greeting and bowing politely to his fans but those boys came to him, he smiled at them.

LET ME HEAL YOU

"You guys are so good", Jimmy said with full admiration in eyes. They were looking at him with shining eyes.

"We are your big fan sir!", One of the boy said.

"I also used to dance here", Jimmy said remembering those days.

"We know sir, You are our Ideal. You are great sir!", The other one said.

"Yes Sir, You are such a inspiration, I want to be like you".

Jimmy paused looking at him; he had never imagined someone saying this to him. He smiled.

"Thank you so much. But don't be like me. Find yourself, trust me you'll be more proud", Jimmy's genuine words really made them smile.

They nodded and bowed. They took pictures with Jimmy and Jimmy went back to Cera who was still sitting in the car with Sarah while looking at him.

Jimmy got into the car and he was silent. Cera smiled and held his hand.

"Jimmy, you should not get out of car just like that. You should be careful", Sarah said but Jimmy didn't say anything as he was still living that moment. Cera chuckled and Sarah sighed and got out of car.

"Umm, Sarah you should leave now. We'll straight go home.

"Are you sure?", Sarah asked and Cera nodded.

"You should let Alex drive", Jimmy said.

"Nah, I'm fine", Cera said and drove off.

And Cera drove.

Jimmy suddenly kissed Cera's hand, she chuckled. Cera didn't say anything and just saw him smiling to himself and living his moment.

It is quoted,

"You don't find love, it finds you"

It has something to do with Destiny and what's written in stars. True love is to see your partner smiling from the far and feel blessed and happy and if they cry, that urge to run to them and pull them in a warm embrace to make them feel safe there.

Love isn't just affection and words, it's sharing of feelings, emotions and hearts, Which Jimmy and Cera got at their first and never let go of it.

The process of healing was slow but they made it.

~The End~

Epilogue

After 5 years :

"AHHHHHH! Cera!!!! Your daughter is GOING WILD LIKE YOU!!", Jimmy shouted.

Cera rolled her eyes hearing her husband as she was busy talking on phone and her husband was shouting in background from living room.

"Umm, Excuse me Mr. John-", She said on phone while walking towards Jimmy but her eyes widened seeing her 4 yos old was pulling Jimmy's hairs while sitting on his shoulder and he was sitting on the floor all done with his daughter.

"Hey!! You two!! Can't you be silent for a second? I'm talking with client. And what the hell is this Jimmy? Are you A kid? Look at the messy room!!", She said madly looking around.

"What me-AHHHH! Ava! Stop pulling my hairs!", Jimmy was really going through a lot but his wife was just ignoring him

"Papa, I'm just styling your hairs", Ava cutely said again collecting Jimmy's hairs in her small fist tightly.

"Aww, my baby. Go on baby", Cera said blowing kiss to her daughter and walked from there ignoring Jimmy again. Jimmy looked at her in disbelief.

"WHAT? Cera, she'll pull out my hairs", He said but...

"Baby, don't pull out all", Cera said while going inside.

"Ok Mama", Ava said and again started to pull his hairs.

Cera had also started her own business, she had her own cake brand which had become very popular because of it's unique taste and Cera's dedication.

And about Jimmy, he was a super star, he had his own unique glow within those shining things around him, he was on the top of the crown, finally there where no one could hurt him anymore. His group had the biggest fanbase globally, his fans' love and family support gave him huge success in his life and he was so satisfied with his life, with his small happy family but.....

"Ahhk- No, Ava, come here baby", Jimmy stopped her and pulled her down from his shoulder.

"See baby, it hurts when you pull Papa's hairs. And if you keep pulling my hairs like this, then I'll go bald honey", He said while almost crying but she giggled covering her mouth with her small hand. Jimmy chuckled on her cuteness.

"I'm sorry Papa. But you'll look funny", Ava laughed.

"Laughing, Huh? You little monster", Jimmy started to tickle her and they both were giggling and laughing.

"Ahh! HAHAHAHAHA! Stop! HAHAHA!", She said laughing breathless. Jimmy smiled looking at her tearing eyes. She was panting Jimmy kissed her cheek.

"Ok, I'll fix it", She said and again started to fix his hairs.

Jimmy was just admiring her with small smile. Ava was just like Cera, Cute, pretty, lovely, evil and stubborn but Jimmy's whole world was in her. When Ava was born, he once again got new life as a father.

"Owk- I forgot to tell you, our drawing teacher Miss. Sana asked me for your number", Ava said innocently but Jimmy eyes slightly widened.

"No baby, You shou-"

"No need to give his number to anyone! You got it?", Cera interrupted him after hearing her daughter. Ava went to Cera.

"No Mama, I didn't give.....I know we need to protect Papa", Ava said but she whispered the last line that made Cera laugh. Cera picked Ava.

Jimmy was curious as Cera suddenly laughed, "What did she say?"

"Jimmy, Our daughter is growing so well", Cera said still laughing.

Jimmy smiled and took Ava from her, "Yes! Because she is my baby!"

"Oh really? But someone was yelling few minutes ago 'Cera!!!! Your daughter is GOING WILD LIKE YOU!!'", Cera said imitating Jimmy and they laughed.

DingDong

They looked at door as the doorbell rang. Cera went to open the door. She opened the door and smiled.

"Hi Lexi, please come in", Cera said welcoming Lexi and her son.

"And What's up Handsome?", Cera said to her son Dooly who was same age as Ava.

Jimmy saw them and kept small smile. Lexi and Rocky had got married and had an adopted son. They were Jimmy and Cera's neighbors. Even though Jimmy didn't want to be with Lexi but she couldn't let go of her only friend just like that, they didn't mean to bother Jimmy, so that bought house near his but not that close. Cera was casual, she knew what trauma Lexi had given to Jimmy. But Lexi also had to go through enough karma. Cera's personality was like that, she forgot everything from past and started with new, accepting present.

"Hi aunty, Uncle Jimmy!", Dooly ran to Jimmy and gave him high-five.

"Hey Champ! How are you?", Jimmy said gladly picking him up as Dooly was enough closer to Jimmy than his parents and was also Ava's friend.

"I'm fine uncle"

But Then Cera noticed Lexi's silence. She was not jolly as usual.

"Cera, will you please let Dooly stay here? I need to go somewhere urgent. I'll be back in two hours", Lexi said.

"Yea sure, why not? But what happened? Where ar-", Cera saw Lexi's falling tears.

"Hey, Lexi", Cera held her hand and looked at Jimmy.

"Hey, What's wrong?", Jimmy asked. Lexi looked at her son and Jimmy got it.

"Bub, go and show Dooly your new car. Go to your room and play. I'll bring snacks for you later", Jimmy said to Ava and both the kids ran into room.

And Lexi broke into tears.

"Lexi, Here sit. What happened? Why are you crying?", Cera asked Lexi. Jimmy brought water for her but she didn't drink.

"Did you hear about Fire accident in IFC building this morning?", Lexi asked while crying.

"Y-Yeah, I saw the news about it", Cera said.

"Yesterday, Rocky had meeting there. But he has not come home yet. His phone is off, I'm scared", Lexi cried.

Cera and Jimmy also looked at eachother worriedly.

"I was going to check him.... What if he-", Lexi couldn't complete and again started to cry.

"No, calm down. Don't think like that. Let's go and see", Jimmy said.

"No, I will go with her. If someone sees you there then, that will be trouble. Stay with kids we'll be back", Cera said.

"Ok and tell me the situations there. I'll inform Officer Reid, He'll help you", Jimmy said, Cera nodded and left from there with Lexi.

Jimmy sighed.

After sometime :

Jimmy was waiting for Cera or any call from her. He was checking his phone again and again. He tried to call her but she was not answering.

But then doorbell rang. Jimmy hurriedly went to open the door thinking it might be Cera but when he opened the door a huge smile came on his face seeing the person after so long without having any contact.

"Harold", Jimmy was about to hug him but then he saw Harold was not alone but someone was with him.

"Hello", Mr. Ford said with small smile. Jimmy gulped nervously not knowing why he was there.

"May we come it?", Harold asked. Jimmy snapped back.

"I-I'm sorry, please come in", Jimmy said moving away and they came inside looking around.

Harold smiled, "Congratulations! I knew it! Your hard work paid off. You guys are everywhere craz! So proud of you". Harold hugged Jimmy.

"Thank you so much Harold", Jimmy said smiling at him.

They sat on the couches. Mr. Ford was not saying anything but was looking around, like finding someone. Harold noticed it.

"Where is C-Cera?", Harold asked.

"Umm, she is not home. She went out for some work. But she'll come back soon. What would you like to have?", Jimmy asked politely. It was so awkward for him.

"No, it's ok. I just came to meet Cera", Mr. Ford said.

Silence……

"Papa, I want some crackers. I want to eat and I broke it again. Will you-", Ava said coming from room but stopped seeing some guests. She smiled at them that made them smile too. She went to Jimmy.

"Our daughter, Ava", Jimmy introduced Ava.

Mr. Ford's heart skipped beats and tears filled in his eyes.

"Papa, who are these uncles?", She whispered to Jimmy but silence was enough to let them hear what she said.

Mr. Ford chuckled, "Grandpa....? I'm y-your grandpa".

She smiled brightly and looked at Jimmy, Jimmy couldn't help but smile.

"Are you really my grandpa?", Ava asked to make sure.

"Yes, Come here", Mr. Ford said and Ava ran to him. He hugged her and tears fell from his eyes. He started to get all memories from Cera's childhood while holding her daughter.

"Grandpa, where were you these many days? I missed you so much. Now I'm mad!", Ava said innocently with mad pout.

"Ayy! I'm sorry baby. You are just like your Mum", Mr. Ford said adoring her.

"Huh- You know my Mom? But you have not met her yet....", Ava said Mr. Ford again chuckled seeing that cute confusion on her face. Harold was just looking at them as he knew something that Cera needed to understand about Mr. Ford.

"I know your Mom because I'm your Mama's Dad", Mr. Ford answered but.....

"Ohhh", She said still with that confused face.

"Ava, see I made this-", Dooly came and he also stopped seeing unknown people. And walked to Jimmy.

"Is he also-"

"Umm, No. He is our friend's son and Ava's friend, Dooly", Jimmy introduced and took Dooly on his lap.

"Hello", Dooly did with a small wave and they smiled.

Jimmy saw how happy Mr. Ford was while talking with Ava.

"Grandpa, come, I'll show you my new car and toys", Ava said holding his hand and started to drag him to her room and Mr. Ford also gladly went with her.

"Hey champ, why don't you join them?", Jimmy asked to Dooly but Dooly turned around and hugged Jimmy.

"When will Mom come?", Dooly asked and Jimmy could feel that he was on verge to cry.

"Hey, Don't cry man. She just went for shopping with aunty. She'll come back. You are hungry, right? Let's get snacks for you", Jimmy said and got up. Harold was just looking at the kid curiously.

"Harold, will you please wait? We'll get some snacks and come back, Ok? Let's GOOO!", Jimmy said and ran to kitchen to make the kid smile.

After few minutes they came back.

"I'll give this to Ava", Dooly said and went inside to share his snacks with his friend.

"Seems like you are doing well so I don't need to ask I guess", Harold said and Jimmy just smiled.

"Yes, what about you?", Jimmy asked.

"Everything is fine, Me and Dr. Lia got engaged last month", Harold said.

"Oh great! Congratulations. I'm happy for you", Jimmy said.

"Sorry for interrupting your happy life like this", Harold said looking down.

"No, what are you talking about? I'm so happy to see you again after years", Jimmy said.

"But Uncle....", Harold said but Jimmy had nothing to say on that.

"He is so guilty about his deeds in past. He is regretting so much. He is missing Cera. It's not like he had some loss in business or something.... nothing. He has everything, may be more than before but not his family, his daughter..... Someone to love him.... He is lonely....", Harold was not sure if Jimmy was understanding but he was trying best to make him understand so that he would make Cera understand the same thing.

"His loneliness is eating him internally. He was not daring to say it but today he told me that he wanted to meet Cera. So I brought him here", Harold said.

"It's ok Harold. I'm happy. We have moved on with our life and stable, I don't mind anything. I have also forgotten everything but I can't say anything about Cera", Jimmy said.

Again, doorbell rang.

"I think it's Cera", Jimmy said and went to open the door.

Jimmy opened the door and saw Cera, Lexi with Rocky. Jimmy sighed. They came in.

"Jimmy, do you know, this guy was drunk last night and was with his friends at their house and here his wife was worrying for no reason, seriously?", Cera said coming inside. She had not noticed Harold yet.

"Oh C'mon Cera, now how many times are you gonna taunt me like this?", Rocky said and they also came in.

"Shut Up! Just look at her", Cera said, Rocky looked at Lexi with puppy face who was glaring at him already.

"Sorry baby, I won't do it again", Rocky apologized to his wife.

"Don't talk to me", Lexi said madly and looked away.

Cera chuckled, "You guys are reall-", and here she saw Harold and her laugh and even that smile faded.

Suddenly that fear of being happy took over her, she gulped and looked at Jimmy, "What is he doing here?" She asked coldly.

Jimmy was about to say but....

"Why are you asking him? Ask me, talk to me", Harold said trying to talk with her.

"I don't want to", Cera said giving Harold cold stares.

Rocky and Lexi were just standing there not knowing what's going on but then.....

"Grandpa, do you have doll house like I have? Then only I'll come with you", Cera heard Ava and turned around just to see Mr. Ford was coming out of room while carrying both the kids.

"Yes, I have everything for both of you. You can come anytime you-", Mr. Ford stopped speaking when he saw Cera and smiled.

"C-Cera....."

But he knew what's coming next.

"Mom-Dad", Dooly said, as soon as he saw them and getting down from Mr. Ford he ran to his dad, Rocky picked him up. And awkwardly looked at Cera.

"Umm, we'll leave now. Bye", Rocky said as it was awkward to interrupt family matter and they left from there.

And here Cera's heart was shaking seeing her daughter in his arms. Shiver ran to her spine making her anxious for some reason. She felt like he'll hurt her daughter. Cera went to him madly and literally snatched Ava from him.

"Mama, see he said, he is my grandpa", Ava said innocently but...

"NO! he is not!", Cera said glaring at him. Tears were already flowing from her eyes.

Mr. Ford's heart clenched hearing her.

"Don't dare to touch my daughter ever again!", Cera said in warning tone being all red in anger.

"Cera, list-", Jimmy tried to speak but

But Cera interrupted him, "Why are these people here? Why did you let them in?"

"Mama, he is my grandpa. Why are-"

"SHUT UP AVA! DON'T YOU UNDERSTAND? HE IS NOTHING TO YOU!", Cera yelled, Ava flinched and started to cry.

"Cera, Why are you shouting on her?", Jimmy said taking Ava from Cera to calm her down.

Cera also started to cry, "Then why doesn't she understand? I'm telling her not to keep any relation with strangers".

Cera's words were stabbing Mr. Ford but he knew he deserved this.

"She is kid, Cera", Jimmy said while trying calm Cera.

"Cera, Please listen to-", Mr. Ford said but...

"GO FROM HERE! LEAVE! DON"T EVER COME AGAIN! Or.... Or else I'll do s-something to myself! I'm Warning You!", Cera cried out loud.

"Cera! What nonsense are you talking infront of kid? Calm down, please", Jimmy said. Cera looked at Jimmy with pleading eyes, asking him to understand her. Jimmy was understanding, he could see how scared and hurt she was but she was completely losing it.

Cera took Ava from Jimmy and stomped towards her room.

"Cera..? Cera-", Jimmy tried to stop her but she left.

Jimmy didn't know what to say as he could see Mr. Ford was hurt too.

"I-I....Umm, I-I'm sorry sir, it-", Jimmy said.

"It's ok, I know it's going to happen anyways. I don't deserve to be forgiven. Today also I came here being selfish, I was missing her because I was alone. But meeting Ava, it made my day. Thank you", Mr. Ford said. "Poor kid got scolded because of me. take care of her", Mr. Ford's feet were too heavy to step out from there.

"I'll leave now, I'm happy to see you all happy and well settled in your life. I won't b-bother you again. I'm sorry for everything.... Everything......", Mr. Ford said while controlling his breaking voice but tears were falling from his eyes.

"Just tell Cera that, I'm really guilty for always hurting her. Tell her not to forgive me but at least come to see me when I die", Mr. Ford broke into sobs. Jimmy felt bad for him.

"S-sir, I can understand you are guilty, don't say like this. But Cera also had to go through some hurtful things that she didn't deserve and you had given some deep wounds which are not easy to heal", Jimmy tried to explain Cera's side to them.

Wounds
SHE ALSO HAD......

"I Know...", Mr. Ford said and turned to leave.

"Sir..."

Mr. Ford stopped but didn't turn.

"You c-can come to meet Ava w-whenever you want.....", Jimmy said but he was still not sure about Cera's decision.

Mr. Ford turned around and hugged Jimmy, tears were again falling from his eyes. Jimmy was hesitating but put his hand on his back.

"Thank you", Mr. Ford moved from the hug wiping his tears.

"Take care", Harold said and hugged Jimmy and left from there with Mr. Ford.

Jimmy sighed and looked towards his room and went to check on Cera.

"I'm sorry baby", Cera was still crying while hugging Ava who was sleeping. Cera put her on bed and felt so bad that she fell asleep while crying, she kissed her head.

LET ME HEAL YOU 285

Jimmy was looking at her from the door. She saw him but again started to cry more. She needed him to embrace her right now, Jimmy came to her and she hugged his waist and cried.

"Why is he here now? W-what does he want?..... I'm happy with my life, h-he can't even see that", Cera was broken.

"Shuu! calm down", Jimmy was caressing her to calm her.

"I shouted on my daughter because of him", Cera was feeling bad.

"Cera, H-He was here to meet y-you", He said. Cera moved away and Jimmy sat near her.

"Why? What's wrong with him now?", Cera was so disgustly in disbelief. Then Jimmy told her what Harold told him about Mr. Ford.

"I'm not surprised Jimmy and not even feeling any sympathy for him. Because he is being served by his karma", Cera said like emotionlessly but Jimmy was not like that, he always flew with emotions. He was feeling bad for Cera as well as for Mr. Ford also because he had seen that guilt and helplessness in Mr. Ford's eyes.

Jimmy held her hand, "Look Cera, however he was but now he is guilty. He is regretting and asking for a chance. You are not like this Cera and in this stage he nee-"

"How can you say like this? Have you forgotten? He didn't show a bit of care or any mercy while making me to abort my first child!! How can I forgive him just like that? When he had me, he never cared. I always did everything for his affection and love but he didn't care about my existence and now after so many years suddenly he shows up just because he's alone, so he wants me and my daughter to entertain him....? NO! Never! I will not bear him near my daughter!!", Cera said madly explaining him as she knew Jimmy was thinking emotionally.

"But Cera, we are happy with Ava, we –"

"But Ava can't fulfill the loss I had Jimmy, I lost someone like Ava. That's nothing to you because only a mother knows that pain!"

Jimmy's Heart shook hearing her, now he was understanding how deep it was. How broken Cera still was. He immediately pulled her in hug when he started to feel her pain.

"Even that thought scares me...... I'm sorry", Jimmy closed his eyes, hugging her tighter.

"I'm s-so sorry Cera, I couldn't understand you. Don't cry, let's just forget whatever happened today, Ok? Now think about how you are going to get forgiveness from Ava. She will be mad", Jimmy said moving Cera away and wiped her tears.

They looked at their daughter and for their surprised she moved in sleep and woke up. They smiled, she looked at both of them but got up and climbed on Jimmy and hugged him resting her head on his shoulder. Yeah she was mad on Cera.

"Ava, Let's go to park today. We will take Dooly and Haru also with us. Sounds fun, right?", Cera said but Ava didn't say anything. Cera looked at Jimmy on verge to cry again.

Cera again took deep breath, "Umm, how about giving a princess a hug-"

"Papa, I want to go out", Ava said to Jimmy.

"Oh Ok", Jimmy said and took her out. Cera followed them.

"Baby, I'm sorry. I didn't mean, I-I won't do it again", Jimmy was walking around with Ava while Cera was following him. But Ava was saying nothing.

"Jimmy! Stay at one place!", Cera said frustratedly.

"Ok, Ava will forgive you, if you catch us. Ok baby?", Jimmy said making Ava smiled.

"Ok!", Ava said and Jimmy winked at Cera and started to run around the house with Ava.

"Papa run!!Papa Run! AHHHh!! She is near! Papa run! HA-HAHAHAHA!! Mama you can't catch me!", Ava said while laughing, Cera sighed looking at her smile that finally something came up.

"Hey! You little! Come here-", Cera was chasing them.

Their house was filled with their laughs.

"Caught You!", Cera finally caught them. "Now where are you going to run?", Cera said hugging Ava.

They plopped on couch catching breath. "Am I forgiven?", Cera asked.

Ava looked at Jimmy and he nodded, she smiled at Cera, "Yes Mama!" Ava kissed her Mom. Cera felt so full while holding her daughter.

Suddenly Ava paused looking at Cera.

"I'm sorry Mama, did I make you cry?", Ava asked and cupped her mom's face with her small hands. Cera shook her head and hugged Ava.

"Nope! You always make me happy hon", Cera kissed her head. Jimmy pulled both of them in his arms.

While they were having their family moment, Jimmy's phone rang. He moved little and answered but his eyes widened hearing from otherside. Cera noticed.

"What?", Jimmy was talking on phone. Cera moved away being worried as he seemed little panic.

"Ok, we are coming", Jimmy said and hung up.

"What happened?", Cera asked.

"It was mom, Emma is in labour and mom wants us to come to the hospital", Jimmy said getting up and went to his room hurriedly to change.

"What? Where is Jack?", Cera asked going behind him.

"That idiot fainted in the labour room!", Jimmy said, he was not so surprised knowing his friend very well.

"What The-....Ahem", Cera gulped on her words as Ava was with her but...

"Fuck!", Ava said.

Silence.....

Jimmy looked at his wife being done and continued to wear his clothes.

"Ayy! It's a bad word", Cera whispered to Ava.

"I'll talk with the doctor in charge, Get ready", Jimmy said And went out. Cera smiled, she was happy for Emma and Jack.

"Where are we going Mama?", Ava asked.

"We are going to have a small baby Ava! Yeayy!"

"Really Mama? Yeayyyyyy!" They both started to dance.

"Yes! But We need to leave girls!", Jimmy said coming in and chuckled seeing them excited but they were getting late.

Milton Keynes UK
Ingram Content Group UK Ltd.
UKHW020908111124
451035UK00018B/1481